Essentials of Literacy
from **0-7** Children's Journeys into Literacy

Tina Bruce and Jenny Spratt

Los Angeles | London | New Delhi
Singapore | Washington DC

First published 2008
reprinted 2009

SAGE Publications Ltd
1 Oliver's Yard
55 City Road
London EC1Y 1SP

SAGE Publications Inc.
2455 Teller Road
Thousand Oaks, California 91320

SAGE Publications India Pvt Ltd
B 1/I 1 Mohan Cooperative Industrial Area
Mathura Road
New Delhi 110 044

SAGE Publications Asia-Pacific Pte Ltd
33 Pekin Street #02-01
Far East Square
Singapore 048763

Library of Congress Control Number: 2007939397

British Library Cataloguing in Publication data

A catalogue record for this book is available from
the British Library

ISBN 978-1-84787-241-8
ISBN 978-1-84787-242-5 (pbk)

Typeset by C&M Digitals (P) Ltd., Chennai, India
Printed in Great Britain by Ashford Colour Press Ltd
Printed on paper from sustainable resources

Essentials of Literacy
from **0–7** Children's Journeys into Literacy

Contents

Introduction and Acknowledgements

> Every few years, there seems to be a passionate debate about literacy in England. Why? There are all sorts of reason for this.
>
> - Governments fear that unless workers are literate, England will not be able to compete in the world with other countries (Brown, 2007).
> - Experts in literacy or aspects of literacy, often believe children are badly taught, because different methods are favoured from the ones they advocate. They seek to influence official approaches to literacy, with the result that across the years there has been great variety as different approaches gain the upper hand (Bullock, 1975; Literacy Hour, 1998; Rose, 2007).
> - Parents, grandparents and the public in general become very confused by all the different 'expert' views on how children should be taught to read and write.
> - Practitioners rarely engage in all the battles about literacy, but they do find it difficult to know, among all the experts, who to trust and who is 'right'. They just want to do their best for the children and families they work with.

Who knows what about literacy – and who is 'right'?

When interconnected knowledge and understanding work in close harmony with tried and tested practice wisdom, then practitioners and parents work well together. The result is that children flourish in their development and learning.

To bring this about, practitioners need regularly to review and reflect on practice, and to see whether it is in tune with new developments in the understanding of both child development and subject knowledge. Inevitably, we find that we need to make some adjustments and changes.

But the changes need to be interconnected to make a consistent, logically coherent whole. If we are totally disconnected from what we have previously known, we shall be in a muddle, unable to see clearly the best ways of linking to what is new.

Becoming a community of learners, adults and children together

The government, since May 1997, as Michael Barber (Stannard and Huxford, 2007: 3) set out in his book, *The Learning Game*, has had an ambition to eliminate failure through:

- guaranteeing standards in the basic skills
- the idea of the school (or early years setting) as a learning institution
- a learning promise to every child
- the wider aims of creating a learning society
- opportunities for lifelong learning.

A decade later, because of a resurgence of interest in the teaching of reading owing to the Rose Review, 18 local authorities accepted the invitation to participate in the Department for Education and Skills (DfES) National Pilot of Early Reading Development (DfES, 2005b), which was based on exploring a systematic approach to the teaching of phonics.

Working together – the first year

For a year, the authors and the teachers in the pedagogy team in one of the 18 local authorities worked with practitioners in the private, voluntary and independent (PVI) sectors. The settings were chosen because they linked into primary schools that the local authority had selected to take part in the DfES project.

The Head of Early Years and Childcare decided the work should develop over two years (rather than the one year of the DfES pilot). Since then she has, with her team, organized a third year of training to share the work we did together across the whole PVI sector, with receiving schools invited to join in.

Working together – the second year

During the second year of our work together (2006), the *Early Years Foundation Stage* (EYFS) was finalized (DfES, 2007a), becoming the legally enshrined official curriculum for children from birth to 5 years of age in England in September 2008. It is this document which guided those taking part in the renamed Communication, Language and Literacy Development Project.

The early years literacy specialist from the Learning and Standards Team in the local authority was formally invited to join the project and, by the summer, reception teachers and year 1 teachers were linking and attending meetings, and asking to be included in the third year of the training.

Working together – the third year

The practitioners who have participated in the first two years are helping us main-stream the training by talking about their work, and encouraging visits from the new participants, so that everyone can learn from each other. Teachers in reception and year 1 classes, encouraged by those who attended the training at the end of the second year, have requested to join us. The leading teachers, with their team leader from Learning and Standards have, to our delight, asked to participate again.

This book is about our work together. We are interweaving the principles, themes and commitments of the *EYFS* with traditional early childhood approaches, and adjusting practice as we respond to recent research on communication, language and literacy.

Into the future, taking treasure from the past and adding new knowledge

We locate Communication, Language and Literacy in a multi-sensory, rich communication and language environment, nesting phonics within that as one aspect of it. We had to do some thinking, and to adjust in order to update our practice without throwing away treasure from the past that needed to be kept. The principles held, but we could see that the practice needed to develop.

We acknowledge the kind permission of the Department for Children, Schools and Families (DCSF) in allowing us to quote in full (see p. 23) the early learning goals for 'Communication, Language and Literacy' (DfES, 2007a: 13) from the Statutory Framework for the *Early Years Foundation Stage*.

Introducing the community of learners

- The authors – Jenny Spratt, Head of Early Years and Childcare in the local authority and Tina Bruce, the external Early Childhood Consultant.
- Contributions were made by the Early Years and Childcare Team members led by Susan Cary and Karen Hingston. They were Jacki Yetzes, Emma Brader, Lesley Evans (part-time), Julia Robinson, Andrea Gamman, Alii Collier, Kim Neilson, leading the training on 'Communicating Matters' (DfES). Heather Fry, speech and language therapist with the Early Years Inclusion Team, Alison Wallace, Alison Riley, Emma Woollard, Steve Wells, Sallyann Hilliard, Annie Hornsby, Jo Smith, Syreeta Payne, Catrina Storey, Cathy Ruffles, Gill Davies, Zelda Eldred and Marilyn Rogers.
- Janet Lavender and Tricia Shingles (music input) were also contributors from the sector.
- Research partners (as the teachers working with the settings were called) were: Margaret Emerson and Cathy Ruffles, Sally Atkinson, Helen Norris, Gill Roberts, Susan Cary and Alison Carroll.
- Seven voluntary managed playgroups participated:

Glinton Pre-School Playgroup, Supervisor Jane Ringham and Leigh-Anne Goodliffe (pre-school assistant)

Helping a child overcome fear of spiders through a project around the rhyme 'Incy Wincy Spider' gives the language of feelings

New Ark Playgroup, Supervisor Elizabeth Buck and Linda Wilson, deputy supervisor

The emphasis on the outdoor area in this setting (where staff are trained in the forest school approach) led to children being encouraged to have phone conversations out of doors. This especially attracts boys, who enjoy chatting in this way

Orton Wistow Under Fives Playgroup, Manager Donna Pickavance

Sharing learning and sustained conversations between parents, practitioners and children who know each other well

Noah's Ark Pre-School, Manager Jacqueline Weaver

Home-made props engage the children, and the staff. Here they are used out of doors

South Bretton Pre-School – Middleton, Manager Judy Flynn

Using small world 'menu' cards, so that children can use these with props in their spontaneous play

Parnwell Pre-School, Jan Jukes

Real experiences support the words of the rhymes and poetry cards, and make sense and meaning for children, who may well not know what pease pudding is, and who may never have seen a pig or a market. Giving meaningful experiences is an important essential of literacy

Rainbow Pre-School, Manager Janice Foulkes Arnold

Story boxes and props for free flow play scenarios are an invaluable resource for practitioners to build up. They encourage children to revisit rhymes and poetry cards, and to vary the themes and create their own. The props help children not to lose the plot or the words of the rhyme as part of a multi-sensory and rich enabling environment

One childminder (in the Childminder's Network), Julie Brown

Mark making – the beginning of letters in his name

Broad rich learning is emphasized. Children often choose to paint or make models of characters such as Humpty Dumpty

Caverstede, a maintained nursery school in the LA (which is also a children's centre). Lucy King and Nicole Gough, a teacher and nursery nurse team. See photo above left

- During the second year we were joined by Mary Purdon (Learning and Standards), who, with her team of leading teachers, Carly Tilney, Linda Harries and Kathryn Gray, worked closely with us, the reception classes and year 1.
- At the end of the second year, the majority of the teachers in reception and year 1 joined us (Samantha Keene from Parnwell Primary School, Jo Simpson from Newark Hill Primary School, Tracey Petherick from Queen's Drive Infant School, Karyn Hillier from Peakirk-cum-Ginton Primary School), Carly Tilney and Linda Harries from Orton Wistow Primary School. They asked to be included in the future training we have developed for the third year.

The importance of a rich language environment, with multi-sensory experience

Boys engaging with early communication, language and literacy

It is interesting that the local authority has an unusually high number of summer-born boys, and we were concerned that they should not be put under inappropriate pressure to read and write. We have therefore emphasized the importance of:

- movement experiences (Greenland, 2006)
- three-dimensional props
- real experiences relating to the props for rhymes.

We found that boys were becoming more interested and involved in aspects of the development and learning relating to literacy and literature.

We hope that from now on, with more practitioners joining the training, and with greater links with the reception and year 1 teachers, we shall take this work forward with positive effect. By this, we do not mean we want children to start reading and writing earlier and earlier. We mean that we have been delighted by the way boys and girls are engaging with and enjoying communicating, developing language, and developing the essentials of reading and writing, hopefully as lifelong pursuits.

A broad, rich and deep curriculum, across all areas of development and learning

Given that all areas of development and learning have equal value in the *Early Years Foundation Stage*, we hope that our work will go beyond narrow literacy training. We are helping children to develop as communicating people, socially and emotionally, creatively, linguistically, physically and in their movement co-ordination, mathematics, reasoning and problem-solving, and knowledge and understanding of the world.

The experiences we are giving the children support learning in all these aspects. Good early childhood practice is not narrow practice. It deepens and expands learning in many ways.

The most reassuring aspect of the Communication, Language and Literacy programme is that children have made the most progress in their phonic development in schools where there is excellent early years provision: where phonics is not taught in isolation but embedded in opportunities to read and write that are meaningful for the children and developed by them.

We are providing them with the tools to communicate, a way of coding what they want to say, but not restricting how or what they do. The writing that children produce is in their own words, not following an adult structure, but reflecting the rich language of their play. These children know that they can communicate, and are confident learners. They are ready to fly! (Mary Purdon from the Learning and Standards Team in the local authority)

By the end of the Foundation Stage, she reported that most children in reception classes were enjoying sharing books, and choosing to look at books with spontaneous interest. They had a good understanding of the alphabetic code, linking sounds and graphemes and were engaged. They came to Key Stage 1 with a real enjoyment of sounds and words, and enthusiastically explored and experimented with these. They are more aware of similarities and differences in sounds and the sources of it than previous groups have been. They have a love of alliteration, rhythm and rhyme.

One of the most important things has been the way the different teams have linked and dialogued together

For the past two years, I have been working in reception classes on the National 'Communication, Language and Literacy Development' programme. I have changed my thinking about children's progress and my expectations of children's achievement in the area of communication, language and literacy. These children from the pre-schools are entering reception with a greater desire to link sounds and letters, engage with rhyming and rhythmic experiences and participate in meaningful mark making. After the initial year, schools were reporting significant gains in many areas, but particularly in linking sounds and letters. With the work being further embedded in the second year these gains seem to have increased. (Leading teacher, Kathryn Gray)

Susan Cary, Manager, Early Childhood Pedagogy

Much of our focus and thinking has been on ensuring a smooth transition for children in reception moving into year 1 in Key Stage 1. With better observation based record-keeping in the EYFS by reception class teachers, which now identifies the phases that children are currently working within in their reading and writing, there can be a smoother transition into Key Stage 1.

Their conversation together echoes Marie Clay:

At entry to school, children have been learning for five years, since they were born. They are ready to learn more than they already know. Why do schools and educators find this so difficult to understand? Teachers must find out what children already know, and take them from where they are to somewhere else. (Clay, 1993: 5)

This means that an understanding from both sectors (schools and PVI settings) of the children and the subject knowledge is required if a true picture of each child is built which will inform the teacher's planning in year 1.

The exchange of information between the settings, schools, parents and carers is essential, sharing examples of work and discussion on individual children's progress.

Karen Hingston, Manager, Early Years Childcare Team

The Communication, Language and Literacy Project has had a huge impact on the way my team and I view our work with early years settings. It has really broadened our view, appreciating it involves everyone and everything that is done within the setting, being integral to all that is provided, the environment, the practitioners and the support they are given. Working together across teams has also had a tremendous impact on developing all our understanding and proved invaluable. We all need to think about what and how we provide for children from the earliest age and the impact this has.

Learning together, adults and children

We are a learning community, in the sense that Michael Barber, (in Stannard and Huxford, 2007: 6) describes. Our training together has led us to the importance of practitioners understanding:

- the biologically driven aspects of child development
- the social and cultural aspects of developing learning
- the subject knowledge practitioners need to enable them to develop the essentials of literacy with other people's children and parents/carers
- the importance of rich learning environments, involving relationships, ideas and feelings as well as the physical sense of self.

In the nineteenth century the educational pioneer Friedrich Froebel created learning communities in his schools in which he advised practitioners and parents, 'Let us live with our children, learning from them as well as teaching them.'

THOUGHTS TO TAKE WITH YOU AS YOU READ THE BOOK

It is likely that experienced practitioners reading the book will find it, in the main, reaffirming. There may be new things to reflect on and consider too, as there have been for us. We have adjusted our practice, but that is part of being in a learning community.

For all practitioners, we hope that we have helpfully captured the excitement of children's journeys into literacy, literature and new knowledge and understanding. The essentials of literacy are about educating children in the deepest sense. We owe it to children to know as much as we can:

- about how children develop and learn
- about how their family and culture and community value literacy
- about acquiring and updating our subject knowledge of what is involved in becoming literate
- about valuing professional development as a key part of this.

Working with other people's children, and their parents, requires us to be as highly trained, educated, measured and mature as possible. All these are parts of the essentials of literacy.

SUMMARY – THE ESSENTIALS OF LITERACY

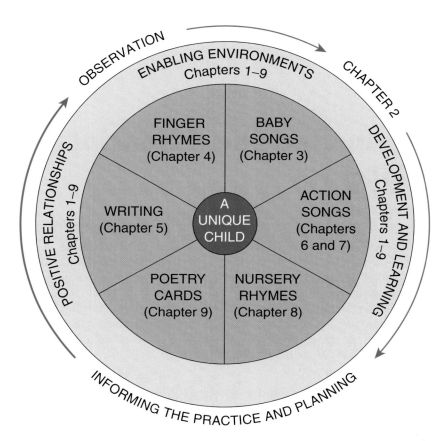

This chart summarizes the book. It shows the areas of communication, language and literacy that we worked on together as a group

Chapter 1

Introducing the Essentials of Literacy

In most cultures of the world, literacy (being able to read and write, either in print or Braille or using computer technological aids) is important and considered necessary for full participation in society, and in order for each person living in that society to make a contribution.

Opening up the world of knowledge and understanding, and finding there is lifelong satisfaction in communicating, with and without words, and in reading and writing, also equips children for survival in a fast-developing global world economy where the future is uncertain and unknown.

It involves:

- good communication (sensitive using words/signs, body language, saying things without words)
- rich language (being articulate and being a sensitive listener)
- becoming a bookworm who avidly reads for pleasure, and information
- writing mainly for pleasure (greetings to family and friends) and other reasons too.

When should children be taught to read and write?

There are various views in different parts of the world about the age at which children should be formally taught to read and write. There are good reasons for this, which we shall explore. In most countries, children are between 6 and 7 years old, because that is a good time biologically, and typically they then learn within about three months. We embrace this in the book.

Do children (provided they are given a good environment) learn to read and write naturally?

One view is that children will learn to read and write quite naturally, but only if they are in an environment which encourages this:

- with people around them reading and writing
- being read to
- engaging with literature and informational print as an important part of every-day life.

Should children learn to read as early as possible?

Another point of view is that children need to be inducted to having the key to a world of literature and knowledge, and to be independent readers as early as possible. Until they can read fluently they are thought to find chunks of text confusing and therefore to be unable fully to appreciate literature or non-fiction texts. The emphasis is on being able to read and write without help (rather than Vygotsky's 1978 notion of practitioners needing to aim at the ripening buds, so that children do not have to perform early, but are supported by adults in their understanding and their competence develops steadily).

Is it important for practitioners to know about the biological, social and cultural development of children, and the subject knowledge of what is involved in literacy, so that they learn how to put the two together in order to help children read and write?

The view of this book is that biologically-driven processes are a vital part of learning to read and write. Without a body and a brain, there is no question of it being possible! But we cannot just leave things to nature. Neuroscientist Colin Blakemore (2001) argues that '**nurture shapes nature**'. This means that there are important processes functioning in the brain, and in the growing and maturing body. If we work with those, we can help children to develop their learning with maximum impact. Our biological selves are shaped and nurtured by people, relationships and culture. This is particularly so where reading and writing are concerned. We are not leaving things to nature. Instead, we are working with nature.

We need to understand what is involved in the subject knowledge of literacy. What are the essentials of texts and how they work? What are the mechanics of reading and writing? Some of the most important things about developing literacy are not always obvious. The way the brain works to co-ordinate vision, hearing and movement is crucial. So is the way the child develops as a symbol maker and symbol user. Talking, understanding what others say, and engaging in conversations are part of this process.

Key moments in the journey towards literacy: walking, talking and pretending

The excitement and celebration of the first steps in walking

When a baby becomes a toddler, and takes his or her first steps, family and friends become electric with excitement. And so they should be. Co-ordination of the body's movements is one of the greatest landmarks towards literacy.

First words

The first time a child very obviously uses a word is of enormous importance in a family. For children who have a hearing impairment, a communication disorder or learning difficulty, this may be a first use of sign language, such as British Sign Language, or Maketon. Words or signs are symbols. They stand for something else, and are imbued with meaning. The words 'Mum' or 'Dad' are not the actual people. They stand for the person, who may or may not be present.

When a child begins to use words and phrases, symbolic thinking has opened up for that child, who can think about the past, present and future, and describe and comment on events and people, expressing thoughts, feelings and developing ideas.

Pretend play scenarios

Some researchers argue that language and other kinds of symbolic behaviours are separate systems. Others argue there are different kinds of symbolic behaviour. You will find, reading this book, that the important thing is to value both the early beginnings and later developments of symbolic behaviour, such as pretend play, drawings and paintings, models, sculptures, dance choreography, musical composition and dramatic play scenarios. The pioneering Italian educator, Malaguzzi (1998), describes these as 'the hundred languages of the child'. We open up a rich world for children when we help them to be symbol users and makers of their own symbols. But we need to remember the warning in relation to the use of the brain: 'Use it, or lose it'.

In order for young children to (later) be able to read and write independently, these are ESSENTIALS OF LITERACY

Literacy has its beginnings in communication and language

Relating to others

- Literacy has its beginnings in social relationships, movement and the senses, communication and language.
- People need to talk with and listen to babies and young children.
- Eye contact with babies is important, and so is looking away when the baby has had enough interacting for the moment.
- Silences and pauses are important. Adults tend to fill silences, when they might be important to leave as moments of reflection and connection.
- Mirroring, turn-taking and imitation are important in developing non-verbal and verbal conversations.

The importance of movement

- As babies crawl, their eyes must move in co-ordinated ways which later track the text on the page. (Greenland, 2006; Bruce and Meggitt, 2007)
- Children need to be able to co-ordinate movements, both large (gross motor) and small (fine motor). The way the eyes, hands, and fingers move together is vital. Arms and shoulders are an important aspect of this. Because of the way the physical body develops, the first parts of the spine to become well co-ordinated are the head and hands. Then the legs become co-ordinated, and walking begins. The arms and legs start to work together. You will see in different chapters of this book that dancing, movement and action songs encourage and support the kinds of physical co-ordination needed to read and write. Unco-ordinated children have great difficulty later when it comes to reading and writing.

Becoming a symbol maker and a symbol user

- Symbols stand for other things and people, both present and absent.
- Personal symbols hold meaning for the child because they are made by the child.
- Texts themselves (the written words) have no meaning. They represent the meanings that are rooted in personal symbols and personal experiences.
- We need to help children develop the essentials of communicating without words. (There is a whole literature, for example, on picture books; see Baddeley and Eddershaw, 1994; Styles and Bearne, 2003; Whitehead, 2007: 46–7, 99–100)
- We need to help children make and use their own personal symbols, relating to their culture and the wider world.
- Music, dance, all the art forms and an appreciation of literature make a huge contribution to the way children develop their understanding and become competent in reading. They give mean-

Picture books are important in focusing children with books

ingful experiences of rhythm, sequence and narrative, tone and intonation, pauses, rhyme and alliteration.
- Order (syntax), sequence and narrative help children to make meaning of texts in stories and poems, to compose their own (fiction and non-fiction) and to understand sentences, beginnings and endings.

The importance of play

Children's spontaneous free-flow play (Bruce, 1991) gives opportunities to use connecting language, to experiment with narrative, characters, revisit songs and rhymes and stories, to make alternatives, to use familiar rhymes, rhythms and alliteration, and to collaborate with others and work as a team to bring about a satisfying play scenario. This works rather in the way of a jazz, drama or dance improvisation.

Play scenario in a café

The importance of conversations with children

- Repeating back, and clarifying, expanding on what children say, helps language to develop.
- Spoken language and the kind of listening that understands what is said, acts on what is said, and responds and initiates, questions and problem-solves, ensures shared sustained conversations (REPEY, 2002).
- Use and understand language or signing for our own thoughts, ideas, feelings and relationships.
- Use and understand language or signing to talk with and respond to other people in all sorts of different situations.
- Children need to be able to understand what is involved in communication without words or sign language. They will not grasp the importance of a question mark if they have not captured the tone and tune of the voice when a question is asked.

Shared sustained conversation leads to deep thoughts

The sounds and subtle messages of non-verbal communications, to do with pauses, the music of anger, lovingly, affectionately muttered sounds, surprise, fear, protective shouts, a sudden look, meeting someone's gaze, or avoiding eye contact, pulling someone to look and share a focus, pointing … Looking and listening, as you will read in this book, are important co-ordinations in the brain. Later when children read and write, the look of the sentences, words and letters will need to co-ordinate with the sound of them in sophisticated ways, which have become internalized processes in tracking, decoding print and encoding the written symbols.

The importance of sounds and listening to them, especially the sounds of languages

- The sounds in the words must be distinguished one from another. The sounds are later mapped onto the letters on the page, and meaning must be there.
- Children need to have developed and learnt spoken or signed language. Many children throughout the world speak two or three languages. Some are lucky enough to speak three languages with entirely different roots and structures (for example, Italian, English and Urdu). This means it is relatively easy to learn any language with ease. Monolinguals have become cut off from the music, phonology (sounds in the language) and forms of all but their own language, and find this more difficult.

Rhythm, rhyme, intonation, alliteration

Distinguishing sounds

- Phonological awareness (the ability to distinguish between similar and different sounds in the language) is crucial to later reading and writing. It is helped when children can hear the differences between phonemes, syllables, initial sounds and rhyming chunks. These terms are all discussed in later chapters of the book.
- Rhythm (music, dance and song) helps children with syllabification, blending and segmentation.
- Tone, intonation and pauses in the language help children to understand punctuation.
- Rhyme helps children to hear the patterns and distinguish between those that sound similar and different, and to see patterns which help them to decode and encode words as they read and write.
- Alliteration helps children to hear the repetition of the smallest units of sound (phonemes) and to see the smallest units of sound in print (graphemes) at the beginning of words.

The boys readily listen to the sounds when rhymes are with action and props

Time-honoured traditions

- Baby songs, action songs sitting on the spot, and later moving from the spot, nursery rhymes, both traditional and modern, and carefully introduced poetry cards help children to put all this together.

- Action songs help co-ordination of sound, vision and body movements. They can be on the spot with upper body movements. They can be moving about using co-ordinated arm and leg movements. All this is important for later reading and writing co-ordination of the senses (including hearing and vision) and the physical body.
- Nursery rhymes and stories help a sense of narrative, storyline and characters, and create events and contexts and new worlds, alternative worlds, imaginative worlds. They help children to engage in 'connecting language' (and, but, then, before, after, soon) (Ragnarsdottir, 2006). They encourage oral and aural blending and segmenting (more of these terms later). This is an aspect of later reading and writing.
- Poetry cards give children opportunities to engage with small manageable chunks of text, to learn about the alphabetic principle and to explore how sounds map onto graphemes (letters or clusters of letters in a word).

The nursery rhyme 'Incy Wincy Spider' is chanted while using the props

Five currant buns in a baker's shop – with evident enjoyment

High well-being

- Ensure the child has high well-being, and is confident enough to problem-solve their way into reading and writing, to have a go, predict, confirm and self-correct. Both beginners and independent readers need to do this. This is very different from guessing.
- Introduce the essentials of literacy at the pace that is comfortable for each child.
- Support and extend the child's literacy learning in the right way for him or her, at the right time, with the child's full and willing engagement.
- Set children on the path to becoming lifelong readers and writers for pleasure, information and understanding from the start, enjoying music, song, dance and sharing books, rhymes and poetry.

The essentials of literacy make it possible for children to:

- read and write with print or Braille
- open up worlds of literature
- open up worlds of knowledge and information

- open up worlds to inhabit through creative writing
- connect with the thoughts, feelings and relationships of others
- connect with their culture and that of others.

Diversity and inclusion

For very good reasons not all children will speak in words, read or write (owing to having complex needs or learning difficulties), but they need to be able to communicate, with or without language or signs. They may enjoy books, drama, music and dance experiences that are found in stories and poems. They may enjoy information books and experiences of nature and everyday life that go with this. The journey into literacy is complex, and cannot be normalized or standardized. One size does not fit all. Although human beings are social beings, they are not herds to be driven.

How to avoid undermining the essentials of literacy

- Encourage **crawling** on the floor.
- Encourage the use of **face-to-face pushchairs**, which give adult and child a shared focus (looking at the same things together), and talking about what you both see, hear, smell.
- Discourage the use of mobile phones on outings and, instead, engage in **talking with** (not at) babies, toddlers and young children.
- The over-use of dummies constrains language development. They can, however, help children with consistently blocked tubes to clear them and be less nasal, hear and sleep better and to be more relaxed and open to learning.
- Do not rush children into formal instruction in reading and writing.

TAKING TRADITIONAL PRACTICE FORWARD IN A LEARNING COMMUNITY

In the chapters that follow, we shall be looking at some traditional ways in which practitioners and parents across the centuries have very effectively and successfully helped babies, toddlers and children to become:

- effective communicators, (spoken and unspoken)
- avid bookworms, mark-makers and writers
- readers at the right time and in the right way for individual children
- seekers of knowledge, understanding and information by sensitive tuning into others, discussion, reading and writing
- appreciators of literature
- on the path to becoming enthusiastic and committed readers and writers for the rest of their lives.

First, we shall look at what is meant by enabling literacy environments indoors and outdoors.

Chapter 2

Observing Children in an Enabling Environment

Observing children is key to supporting and extending the way children make their unique journeys into literacy. Observation informs the planning for individual children and the way adults engage with the group as a whole.

The way adults relate to children, and the enabling environment they create indoors and outdoors are both essential to developing communication, language and literacy.

A rich environment needs constant adjustment, in response to what is observed, but there are also essentials which should always be there.

Observing children

Effective observation informs the way in which we work with children and their families: 'Records are about getting to know the child and what the child needs' (Bartholomew and Bruce, 1993: 100); 'The impact of observational assessment is not measurable by its weight. It is the use to which the practitioner puts their observations that is important' (Creating the Picture, 2007: 8).

Observation helps us to

- find the child's voice through their interests and needs
- track a child's development and learning
- plan for the child in appropriate ways
- keep in mind the whole child
- use everyday situations to assess a child's progress
- work with parents
- work with other professionals
- see the child in different situations across time.

Making a narrative observation

Systems need to be in place so that every child is observed regularly, and observations are shared with parents, who are encouraged to contribute.

- Note the time of day and the date, and the child's age.
- The observer writes briefly about the context of the observation. Indoors? Outdoors? In the sandpit? Eating lunch?
- The observer writes down as exact a description as possible of what the child says and does. If other children are also involved, the observer writes down enough description of the conversations and action of other children to give a clear picture of the child.
- The observation should not be written judgementally.
- The observation can, afterwards, be analysed and interpreted.
- The observation can be linked with the observations of the child made by other people (including parents).
- The observations can inform the planning.

Making an anecdotal observation

Not all observations will be on-the-spot, narrative observations. Some will be anecdotal. This means the practitioner remembers back and notes something afterwards. It is a good idea to use a different coloured pen for narrative observations (say, written in black) and anecdotal observations (say, written in blue).

It is important to find useful lenses through which to analyse observations

There are many different lenses through which to analyse the observations – each useful for different situations and purposes. We used these to help us analyse our observations:

- Well-being Scale (Laevers, 1994)
- Leuven Involvement Scale (Laevers, 1994) (Leuven, 1994) Laevers, F., Vandenbussche, E., Kog, M., Depondt, L. (1994) A process-orientated child monitoring system for young children ('The Leuven Scales'), Experiential Education Series no 2, Centre for Experiential Education).
- Child Engagement Scale (for children birth to 3 years) (Pascal and Bertram, 2006) Connectedness, Exploration and Meaning Making
- Twelve Features of Play (Bruce, 1991, updated on pages 28–9)
- *Early Years Foundation Stage* (DfES, 2007a) areas of Development and Learning.

Children engage with their learning

Many nurseries now have the children's folders, with photographs, examples of drawings and written examples, available for the children and families to view

Free flow play (Bruce 1991) using See saw Margery Daw

whenever they would like to (Hutchins, 2006). Being part of a learning community means that the spirit is not competitive or judgemental. Instead, everyone is trying to build on a child's interests and needs.

The only records which are not open are those relating to child protection, containing sensitive data and medical records.

Multi-professional teams working in integrated ways

Practitioners from different training backgrounds emphasize different aspects of the child's growing, developing and learning. This is invaluable. The contribution of health visitors, speech and language therapists, physiotherapists, art therapists, music therapists, psychologists, and so on all give different perspectives, which help teachers and early years practitioners to create a picture of each child.

The Early Years Foundation Stage Profile

By the time they are 5 years of age, many children will not have achieved all the early learning goals for communication, language and literacy. Some of the goals are too challenging, and pressure to achieve them would be inappropriate for many children. It is important to observe and act in the light of observations to support the journey children make towards these goals. Few achieve the goals relating to using sentences and captions.

The Early Years Foundation Stage Profile is based on the accumulating observations and knowledge of the whole child. By the end of the final year of the *EYFS*, the Early Years Foundation Stage Profile provides a way of summing up the child's journey so far. When used appropriately, this is invaluable in helping schools and local authorities to see how groups of children are making progress in relation to national trends. For example, it is possible to break this down to see how girls or boys are progressing. We are only at the beginning of working with the data in the Early Years Foundation Stage Profile, but it is very exciting to see children's learning journeys unfolding, and to see what we can do to make them enjoyable and rich for developing the learning of children in relation to communication, language and literacy.

The EYFSP has huge potential to be used as a tool to promote high quality practice. It can help us to recognise and understand the individual characteristics and talents of a child. This information can then be used to shape our curriculum provision and support the child to take further steps in learning on transition to year 1. (Spencer, Bruce and Dowling 2007: 10)

The early learning goals for communication, language and literacy

Some goals for CLLD are unrealistically challenging so that, by the time they are 5 years old (which means many children will be in year 1 of primary school at this point), only some children will be comfortably and appropriately able to:

- Interact with others, negotiating plans and activities and taking turns in conversation
- Enjoy listening to and using spoken and written language, and readily turn to it in their play and learning
- Sustain attentive listening, responding to what they have heard with relevant comments, questions or actions
- Listen with enjoyment, and respond to stories, songs and other music, rhymes and poems and make up their own stories, songs rhymes and poems
- Extend their vocabulary, exploring the meanings and sounds of new words
- Speak clearly and audibly with confidence and control and show awareness of the listener
- Use language to imagine and recreate roles and experiences
- Use language to organise, sequence and clarify thinking, ideas, feelings and events
- Hear and say sounds in the order in which they occur
- Link sounds to letters, naming and sounding the letters of the alphabet
- Use their phonic knowledge to write simple regular words and make phonetically plausible attempts at more complex words
- Explore and experiment with sounds, words and texts
- Retell narratives in the correct sequence, drawing on language patterns of stories
- Read a range of familiar and common words and simple sentences independently
- Know that print carries meaning and, in English, is read from the left to right and top to bottom
- Show an understanding of the elements of stories, such as main character, sequence of events and openings, and how information can be found in non-fiction texts to answer questions about where, who, why and how
- Attempt writing for different purposes, using features of different forms such as lists, stories and instructions
- Write their own names and other things such as labels and captions, and begin to form simple sentences, sometimes using punctuation
- Use a pencil and hold it effectively to form recognisable letters, most of them correctly formed. (Statutory Framework for the *Early Years Foundation Stage*, DfES, 2007a)

Continuing the learning journey

Transitions   Transitions are important. Good transitions mean there is no loss of learning. Bad transitions mean unhappy children, or children who become unsteady in their learning while they adjust to a new life. The first transition is from home to a childminder or a group setting.

Moving together with friends   Groups of children who move together, from an early childhood setting into a school, seem to achieve better. They have established relationships with other children, which eases the transition and enables them to learn more effectively.

Play props for 'Five freckled frogs' (or is it six?)

Moving to a school where there is good early years practice until children are 7 years old

Children flourish where good early years practice is in place from birth to 7 years, with seamless progression. Marian Whitehead (2007: 79–93) writes about what makes an enabling environment in communication, language and literacy for children up to 8 years.

When we are working with children we need to be on the lookout for moments to record children's progress in a wide range of different aspects of communication, language, and love of literature in fiction, non-fiction reading and writing. This will show itself in their play scenarios, their interest in labels and print in the environment, how they engage with other children and adults, when and how they seek out books, how they play with language, their enjoyment of movement, music and dance, and whether they spontaneously choose to mark-make and attempt to write. As children become older, the detail of what we record needs to track their progress and the help needs to carefully match their needs, and continued engagement with literature and finding out, seeking information and commenting on the world about them as their literacy develops.

Tuning into children means adults know how they feel, think and relate to people, and when they are in or out of their comfort zone. It enables practitioners, working in close partnership with parents and carers, to extend the developing learning of the children they work with in ways and at times that are right for them

Creating the atmosphere

We have seen that it is important for adults to be good observers of children, so that they can respond in supportive ways to the things that worry, interest and fascinate children. Tuning into children means adults know how they feel, think and relate to people, and when they are in or out of their comfort zone. It enables practitioners, working in close partnership with parents and carers, to extend the developing learning of the children they work with in ways and at times that are right for them.

Earlier we saw that literacy rests on linguistic development. Children need to grow up in an atmosphere where there is sensitive non-verbal communication and encouragement to put things into words (or signs). Children talk with us readily about what they find interesting, or what they find surprising. They need explanations and reasons why they cannot do something, or should not have done something, or should do something. They talk with us about stories, models they make, drawings and dances, music and nature in the garden if they find adults are sensitive to their feelings and thoughts, and are genuinely interested.

The adults show genuine interest in the conversations

Giving children time to express their thoughts and feelings in an unrushed atmosphere means:

- Not speaking for the child.
- Talking *with* children, not *at* them.
- Having a conversation, not giving a monologue.
- Giving the child undivided attention.
- Sharing experiences together which are worthwhile.
- Making sure children feel that what they say is valued and appreciated.
- Having conversations face to face with children, not towering above them.
- Following the gaze of a young child to see what they are interested in.
- When not sure what a child says, saying what we think the children said.
- Or asking the child if we are right that they said something.
- Or asking the child to repeat what they said.
- Remembering that conversations are about taking turns.
- Asking questions that help conversations. What now? What if? How does this work?
- Avoid conversation-stoppers by demanding replies, such as when adults ask a question that they already know the answer to, but insist the child answers.
- Finding what interests the child, as they will be more likely to want to talk about their interests.

Conversations

With babies and toddlers we will try to match our actions and what we say with the child's. This echoing, side-by-side behaviour is an important part of communication.

Another important strategy is to rephrase with correct grammar what the child has said. For example, 'I goed out' is rephrased as 'You did go out didn't you?'

When we chat with children, it is important that we have shared sustained conversations (REPEY, 2002). We will need to do this by expanding what the

Matching pictures and words

child says. For example if the toddler says 'gone' we might say, 'Yes! The dog has gone hasn't he?' Helping children to talk so that they go beyond the here and now is important too: what we did, where we will go.

Children readily engage with pleasure and fascination with accents, dialects, rhymes and creoles. All this helps them to work out what is involved in language and literacy, and literature. The diversity of the UK today greatly enhances this possibility.

Play with language and its sounds

Nonsense words that rhyme   Children, as we noted earlier, delight in playing with the sounds and words of their language. They readily make up nonsense words, particularly enjoying making rhyming strings

Matching pictures and words   Children build up a sight vocabulary matching words and pictures in games. This helps later word recognition.

Voice sounds   These often happen quite spontaneously. When Sam saw and smelt the rotten food, nine days old, he uttered a disgusted sound, 'errrrh!' These are moments to capture, as the practitioner did, because she wrote it down. In this way, children begin to use long and short vowel sounds, which will be important as they learn to read. (See page 116).

The (hidden) importance of play

Play opens up the world of literacy in ways which are appropriate and right for young children. Children who do not have opportunities for play with narrative and story-making, with characters and creating places and events, often appear to be making sufficient progress in their reading and writing in Key Stage 1. Hrafnhildur Ragnarsdottir (2006) and her colleagues in Iceland and Norway argue that their research is beginning to show that poorly developing narrative and discourse (connected language) proficiency do not show up on word recognition and word comprehension tests until children are about 9 years old. These children have great difficulty with reading comprehension.

Why narrative (stories, poems and rhymes) supports later word recognition and word comprehension

Children who do not have a good grasp of all these essentials of literacy have difficulty in reading comprehension and writing, but it does not become obvious until they are about 9 years old, according to Ragnarsdottir. Dominic Wyse (2003) also emphasizes a rich literature environment, full of stories and poetry and rhymes.

Ragnarsdottir (2006) emphasizes:

In their play, and through being introduced to rich stories and poems and rhymes in a traditional as well as current range of literature, children develop essentials of literacy they will need for later reading comprehension and recognition

- narrative is important in the literature (stories, poetry, rhymes) we tell and read to children, and get them to act out, re-enact, with small world, dressing-up clothes and so on;
- narrative is important in the spontaneous free-flow play of children, when they make the storyline and the characters who live out the stories they create, often based around stories we have told them, or television and digital versatile disk (DVD) material they have seen at home.

Listening to and making narratives with stories and characters has a long-term impact on vocabulary development and discourse proficiency (the way children connect the words together) in young children. According to Ragnarsdottir, these are essential elements in a child's journey into literacy:

- understanding narrative, and having a storyline with characters
- developing a rich vocabulary, important for reading and writing
- connecting words together, linking different ideas, different places and times, referring back and forward to events, setting the scene, and making characters, being clear for the listener to understand, showing inner feelings of characters, recounting a series of events
- sequencing events in a story
- acting out a story
- being clear enough for the listener to understand the story when retelling a story (this is called theory of mind – getting on the inside of what it is like to be listening to the story and what information that person needs)
- thinking about how to make the listener feel suspense, or feel that the story is convincing
- having enough vocabulary to tell the story
- developing your own 'voice' in telling the story

- phonological awareness
- using connectors to join words with increasing complexity
- setting the scene for the story (and, the, but, here, there, this one, although)
- establishing the characters and introducing them to the listener
- having a starting-point for the story
- developing a storyline or plot
- resolving the story with an ending
- direct speech from the characters in role
- characters who see things from different points of view.

Jumping off Humpty's wall

All these elements develop through the free-flow play of children, and are hugely helpful, these researchers argue, for later skill in creative and factual writing as well as for reading comprehension and recognition. They argue that if these are not in place by about 9 years of age, children are likely to score low in literacy and all school work.

The features of free-flow play
(Bruce, 1991, updated here)

One of the ways practitioners can become informed about children's play is through reflecting on the features of play as it flows.

There are 12 features of play which help practitioners to see a child's developing learning:

Free-flow play with Humpty Dumpty. Using first-hand experience, making up rules, finding props, choosing to play, playing together, owning the play, engaged, showing physical competence, integrating thoughts and feelings around Humpty Dumpty. Probably not pretending, or rehearsing the future. Nine out of 12 features of play are present. This is rich free-flow play

- Look out for the way children use first-hand experiences they have had.
- Note how children stay in control as they play, making up their own rules in order to do so.
- Look at how children make or find play props.
- Children cannot be made to play. They choose to play and cannot do this to order. They choose to join others in play, or to initiate play spontaneously.
- Children rehearse the future as they create role play and possible scenarios.
- Play might involve pretending.

- Children might choose to play alone.
- Children and children, or children and adults might play together, in parallel or co-operatively in pairs or in groups.
- Every player has his or her own personal play agenda, although he or she may not be aware of it!
- Rich play means that a child will be deeply engaged, difficult to distract and wallowing in the play.
- Children try out their latest learning, skills and competencies as they play. Play is not so much about learning new things as celebrating new learning.
- As children play, they co-ordinate their ideas, feelings and thoughts, and they make sense of their relationships with family, friends and the culture(s) in which they are growing up. Play that is integrated in these ways flows along in a sustained way, which is why it is called free-flow play. (Bruce, 1991, updated here)

Mary, Mary, quite contrary How does your garden grow?

Props boxes to support the stories and rhymes

Gathering materials to be stored in a box, so that children can spontaneously create the whole scenario opens up the possibility to act and retell, to make variations on the theme in play.

Dressing up clothes to support the stories and rhymes

Acting out rhymes in real situation

Role play

Revisiting rhymes

Children, spontaneously and creatively making their own props and using them as they sing songs and rhymes or retell stories

Sharing books together, as well as looking at books alone

Children benefit from having a book corner, which needs to be warm, light and cosy. Cushions on the floor cater for lounging with books. A small table and

Dr Foster went to Gloucester
In a shower of rain
He stepped in a puddle
Right up to his middle
And never went there again

Rain, rain go away
Come again another day

chairs are more comfortable for other children, while others appreciate a sofa so that adults and children can be cosy as they share books together.

Children need to be able to choose books to look at and become absorbed in, or to share with an adult, and perhaps one other child. This re-creates the feeling of a bedtime story. It is a relaxed atmosphere, and the child can create dialogue around the text and story or the rhyme in the book.

There should be a good range of books: poetry and rhymes, stories and non-fiction. Books with both the music and songs are very popular. Books made by practitioners with and for the children are much loved by parents and children.

When displays are taken down, practitioners often put them into home-made books for the book corner, where everyone can take trips down memory lane about the experiences they have shared together.

Book boxes

A practitioner in one of the pre-school playgroups said:

> We have always had a wide range of books. We have altered our book corner to extend it with a listening corner, and our writing corner, where children have free access to a wide range of mark-making resources. We have purchased more books, big and small, both fiction and non-fiction to relate to current topics and children's own interests. We have offered books to borrow which has been a success.

Borrowing books

Having a system in place so that children and their families can take books home to enjoy is becoming widespread practice. Older brothers and sisters often enjoy reading to their younger siblings. It is invaluable when children need simple texts, which they might be embarrassed to choose for themselves, but can do so in a relaxed way if they are reading for a younger child.

Sharing a book

Older children reading to younger children

Many schools have special times in the week when older children can enjoy coming into the nursery to share books with younger children. It is especially valuable in supporting children to read more fluently and with more confidence. It also encourages children to read with expression. If they do not, the younger child quickly loses interest. This means that it keeps the reasons for reading at the centre. Without meaning, reading print is pointless for everyone.

Children benefit from being with children who are a few steps ahead of them in their literacy journeys. It helps them to see what is involved, and encourages rehearsal, or seeking help when they need it. Mixed age groups give rich opportunities in this way. Two-year-olds often imitate writing and reading behaviour when they see their 3- and 4-year-old friends engaging in representational drawings, or writing their name, or approximate reading of a rhyme. (Matthews, 2003)

Listening corner

Sometimes children want to listen alone to a story. They are not yet at the point where they can read it for themselves, but they have become aware of the fact that print carries meaning and can be read. It takes the frustration away for beginner readers if they can hear the story read on a tape, and turn the pages of the book as they follow the rhyme. Rhymes are a good way of giving children manageable chunks of text for this purpose. Children often point to the print as they hear the words, and engage in 'approximate' reading as their finger starts at the beginning and ends at the end, but gets a bit lost in the middle. It helps children to understand the importance of following sentences in a text.

The importance of fiction

Stories, poetry and rhyme are time-honoured ways in which children are introduced to culture. Sometimes we tell stories, poems or rhymes without books.

Stories, poetry and rhyme are time-honoured ways in which children are introduced to culture

Sometimes we use books. The oral tradition is more powerful in some cultures than others, but where it is strong there is usually greater participation by people in dance, song, music and drama. Story books need to draw children in when we read to them, but as Margaret Donaldson (1978) suggests, children have not often met the author, and so they are more remote for children. Children need both.

Short stories

Sayings   Marian Whitehead (2007: 33) sees 'sayings' as shared shorthands which people have said, often for centuries, and passed on by word of mouth. Tom, (aged 2 years and 6 months) was at the top of the stairs with his mother and her friend. His mother said, 'I smell a rat'. He started to sniff the air, and went all the way down the stairs, saying, 'I can't smell a rat, Mummy.' This is an example of how a young child is working out what is a real statement and what is a saying.

The adult says to the child trying to zip up his coat, 'Can I help you? We can do it between us. Where there's a will there's a way.' Understanding sayings is part of linguistic development.

Nursery rhymes give children, in a simple form, some of the essentials of literacy. They should never be used in isolation but as part of a rich backcloth of play, first-hand experiences indoors and outdoors, interconnected with every area of development and learning

Rhymes and poems   As the Opies (1988) have shown, nursery rhymes and singing games give children important messages about the history of the culture, and open up opportunities to talk about how things have changed. They provide short chunks of phrases, which children enjoy for their alliteration and patterns of rhyme. An example would be 'Ring a ring o' roses'. This refers to plagues, perhaps referring back to that in the 1390s as well as that in 1665. The roses were the boils on the skin, and the posies were the herbs carried to hide the smell of sickness and were thought to ward off contagion. A saying that goes with this is:

1665, not a soul alive
1666, London burnt to sticks.

Nursery rhymes give children, in a simple form, some of the essentials of literacy. They should never be used in isolation but as part of a rich backcloth of play, first-hand experiences indoors and outdoors, interconnected with every area of development and learning.

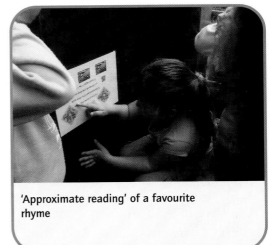

'Approximate reading' of a favourite rhyme

Longer stories

Folk tales, myths and legends It would take another book to do justice to the longer stories we tell children. There are folk tales from all over the world, and they provide a rich form of stories, told orally in their origins, but now written down and presented with beautiful illustrations for children. Favourite folk tales would be *Anansi*, *The Enormous Turnip*, *Chicken Licken*, *The Little Red Hen*, *The Gingerbread Man* and *Babushka*. Favourite myths and legends might include the story of King Midas.

Everyday stories

Children engage with stories about going to see Gran, or going to the shops, making bread rolls, getting wet in the rain. The best of these kinds of stories are often the ones where the practitioners make books for children around particular shared experiences they have together.

Information books

It is often observed that there is a tendency for boys to enjoy looking at non-fiction, information books more than stories. It is therefore very important to have a good balance of fiction and non-fiction books.

Humpty Dumpty play

Non-fiction books to support every part of the enabling environments indoors and outdoors

The book corner is of central importance, but it is also very important to have books everywhere. This can easily become a clutter. It is therefore important to match books to the learning environments indoors and outdoors.

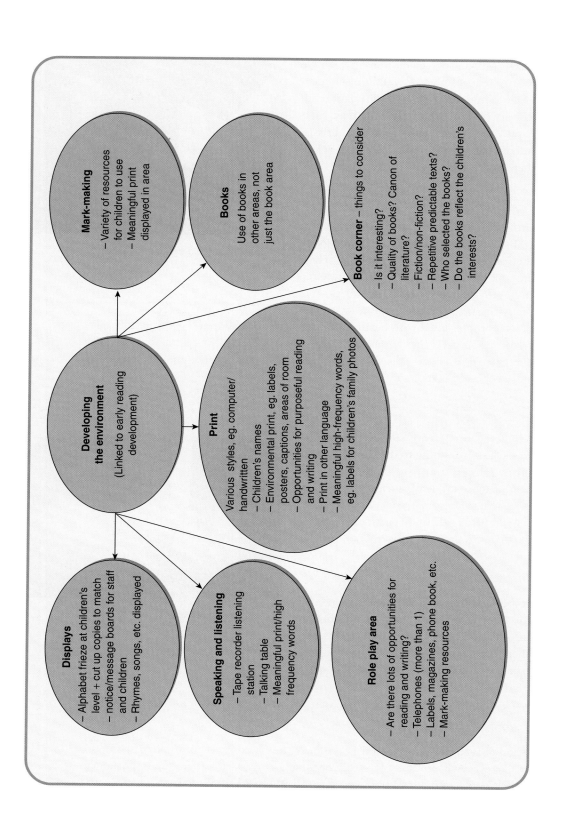

Mark-making
– Variety of resources for children to use
– Meaningful print displayed in area

Books
Use of books in other areas, not just the book area

Book corner – things to consider
– Is it interesting?
– Quality of books? Canon of literature?
– Fiction/non-fiction?
– Repetitive predictable texts?
– Who selected the books?
– Do the books reflect the children's interests?

Developing the environment
(Linked to early reading development)

Print
Various styles, eg. computer/handwritten
– Children's names
– Environmental print, eg. labels, posters, captions, areas of room
– Opportunities for purposeful reading and writing
– Print in other language
– Meaningful high-frequency words, eg. labels for children's family photos

Displays
– Alphabet frieze at children's level + cut up copies to match
– notice/message boards for staff and children
– Rhymes, songs, etc. displayed

Speaking and listening
– Tape recorder listening station
– Talking table
– Meaningful print/high frequency words

Role play area
– Are there lots of opportunities for reading and writing?
– Telephones (more than 1)
– Labels, magazines, phone book, etc.
– Mark-making resources

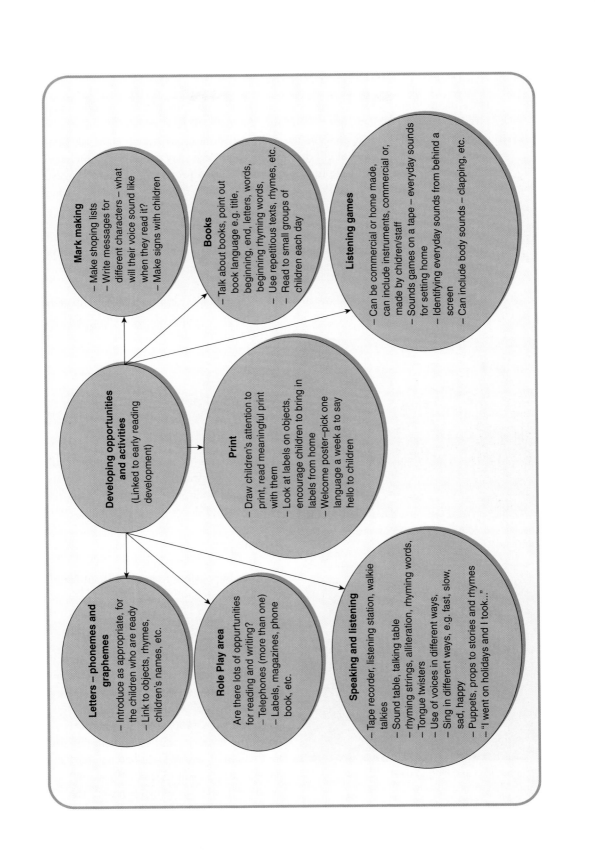

Developing opportunities and activities
(Linked to early reading development)

Mark making
- Make shoping lists
- Write messages for different characters – what will their voice sound like when they read it?
- Make signs with children

Books
- Talk about books, point out book language e.g. title, beginning, end, letters, words, beginning rhyming words,
- Use repetitious texts, rhymes, etc.
- Read to small groups of children each day

Listening games
- Can be commercial or home made, can include instruments, commercial or, made by chidren/staff
- Sounds games on a tape – everyday sounds for setting home
- Identifying everyday sounds from behind a screen
- Can include body sounds – clapping, etc.

Print
- Draw children's attention to print, read meaningful print with them
- Look at labels on objects, encourage children to bring in labels from home
- Welcome poster-pick one language a week to say hello to children

Letters – phonemes and graphemes
- Introduce as appropriate, for the children who are ready
- Link to objects, rhymes, children's names, etc.

Role Play area
Are there lots of oppurtunities for reading and writing?
- Telephones (more than one)
- Labels, magazines, phone book, etc.

Speaking and listening
- Tape recorder, listening station, walkie talkies
- Sound table, talking table
- rhyming strings, alliteration, rhyming words,
- Tongue twisters
- Use of voices in different ways,
- Sing in different ways, e.g. fast, slow, sad, happy
- Puppets, props to stories and rhymes
- "I went on holidays and I took…"

Fiction books with play props

Dressing up clothes and play props can often be a bit random. If stories become much loved favourites, children appreciate having the materials so that they can create play scenarios around them. They will often make variations on a theme (Bruce, 2004a).

The richest play comes if children create their own play props. Having cloaks, a few scarves and hats, basic tunics and open-ended props triggers and suggests ideas to children (Bruce, 2001)

The use of props with rhymes and songs and stories

The possibilities are endless, and a source of rich experiences in communication, language and literacy. They open up the worlds of drama, music, song and dance as well as literature.

The charts (pages 34–5) show different ways of helping children to participate in their culture, and to learn about other cultures in ways which are manageable for them. Children need them all as part of a rich languages and literature environment.

Display should have a clear focus and not be cluttered

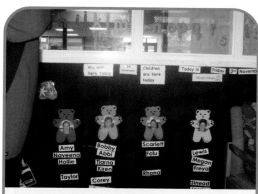

Children need meaningful print, such as their name. Then they are likely to look at it

Meaningful print

Displays – less is more

It is often the case that practitioners fill every bit of wall with print or display, sometimes spilling over and covering the windows and doors.

- This makes children edgy, with an impact on behaviour. It is not calm.
- It is impossible to see the print for all the clutter.

Favourite words – especially the child's name

One of the things we discussed when we met for our training session was the pioneering work of Sylvia Ashton Warner, in New Zealand in the 1950s. She noted and wrote down the favourite and emotionally impor-tant words of the children she taught. Each day, she asked them to read their words, and any they could not remember were thrown away. In this way they built up a sight vocabulary (word recognition) which engaged their interest because it was made up of words that were important to them. Sylvia Ashton Warner understood that reading words needs to engage children's feelings, interests and relationships with people they love as well as their thoughts.

The childminder made a set of 'special words' with her children. They included words like 'plane', 'tiger', 'digger', 'train' and 'dragon' and the child's name. The name was put on the shoe-box in which their special words were kept.

A box of special words for the child

Children's names are important to them as the 'first fixed string' of letters making a word

Names are part of the way children build their identity and they are of emotional importance.

Self-registration

Children find their photograph and put it in a box to show they have arrived. They might also be encouraged to find their name to put next to their photograph.

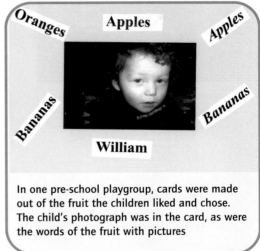

In one pre-school playgroup, cards were made out of the fruit the children liked and chose. The child's photograph was in the card, as were the words of the fruit with pictures

Placemats with the words the child has chosen on them

Noticing letters and words indoors and outdoors

Poetry cards

These give children small manageable chunks of text with large print. Poetry cards are invaluable. These were explored in a later chapter.

Sequencing cards to support children in retelling stories and rhymes

Children mark-making and writing

There should be a mark-making area with a carefully selected and presented range of paper and pencils, felt pens and crayons. It is helpful if this place is near to the workshop area, with scissors, glues, masking tapes, string, hole punchers, etc. Children often want to make cards and books, and need to have the material to do so.

Rory found 'R' for Rory on the outdoor alphabet

This is 'e' for eggs. The chickens on our farm laid the eggs in the photograph

Children can sort out the order of events in a story. Doing this with simple nursery rhymes makes a manageable beginning

'Horsey, horsey don't you stop
Let your feet go clippety clop'
Making and finding musical and rhythmic sounds

The clutter issue raises itself again. Depending on the number of children using the area, it is best to have two of each coloured pencil, a few black-leaded pencils, a few of each size of paper and envelopes, etc. If there are too many, children will not take care of the area and clearing up time becomes a nightmare. If children know where everything goes, and see the labels on pots and baskets, saying '6 black pencils', '4 right-handed pairs of scissors', '2 left-handed pairs of scissors', '3 small envelopes', etc., they are seeing meaningful print which will guide them to put things in the right places. It also helps children ready to do so to read the captions.

Making pease porridge (or pease pudding!)

We looked at some fish

Its along way

Going to the shop is a long way. We looked at some fish

Making the wall for Humpty Dumpty in the garden

Making gingerbread men after hearing the story

Movement, dance and music

The importance of these is woven throughout the book.

Powerful first-hand experiences which support understanding of rhymes

Gingerbread Man

Making a wall   It is a good experience to use three-dimensional props when acting out nursery rhymes. Boys are more likely to become involved. In the photograph above the children are making a wall in the garden. There is a good balance of boys and girls choosing to take part.

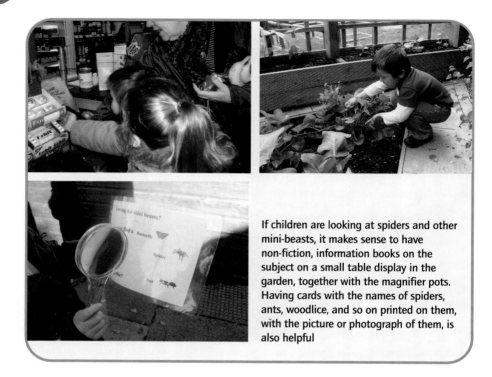

If children are looking at spiders and other mini-beasts, it makes sense to have non-fiction, information books on the subject on a small table display in the garden, together with the magnifier pots. Having cards with the names of spiders, ants, woodlice, and so on printed on them, with the picture or photograph of them, is also helpful

Making an organic garden The children became enthusiastic gardeners in one pre-school playgroup. They linked this with the rhyme, 'Mary, Mary quite contrary'.

Places where people tend to chat and make conversations

Sitting round the fire, cooking dampers, having conversations, exchanging ideas, singing songs, It is a good place to sit and think too

OPENING UP THE WORLD OF COMMUNICATION, LANGUAGE AND LITERACY IN AN ENABLING ENVIRONMENT

Observing the uniqueness of each child's learning journey from birth to 7 years enables us to:

- build on that child's individual interests and needs
- work in partnership with parents and carers, as a team
- explore and track children's progress
- inform our planning, both for individual children and for the group as a whole
- work with other practitioners who are important to the child
- see that children are unique individuals
- see how interconnected the different areas of development and learning are.

In this chapter we have focused on how and what adults need to offer to create enabling environments for rich communication, language and literacy.

Chapter 3

Baby Songs

There is nothing more fascinating than studying children and how they develop and learn. This involves exploring:

- brain development
- how we can help children to connect, communicate and engage with the people they spend time with
- how we encourage children's participation in the social and cultural elements of life through baby songs and finger rhymes.

The development of the brain

People often, mistakenly, believe that brain development is only about the physical development of a child. This is only part of the story. Brain development is also largely about the social and emotional development of children, as well as the increasing ability to think and have ideas (Blakemore and Frith, 2005; Goddard-Blythe, 2004; Trevarthen, 2004).

We need to explore the multi-sensory world of the child as a crucial aspect of learning. We are constantly looking at the importance of sound, sight, feel and touch, smells and tastes and, very important, the movement and feedback from movements made. Penny Greenland (2006) emphasizes the importance of movement as the 'felt sense of life'. Elizabeth Harrison (1895), writing about Friedrich Froebel's early kindergartens, understood the child's need for movement by stating 'the effect of the body upon the mind is not generally appreciated'.

We are beginning to gain a deeper knowledge of the link between the body and the brain, through neuroscience.

An integral part of life from the moment of conception until death, and a child's experience of movement plays a pivotal part in shaping his/her personality, his/her feelings and his achievements. Learning is not just about reading, writing and maths. These are higher abilities that are built upon the integrity of the relationship between brain and body. (Goddard-Blythe, 2004:5)

The first few months – looking, listening and moving

Listening – the beginnings of phonological awareness

Even in the first month, babies react to sounds around them, loud sounds, particular music, the voice of their parents and close family. This will be important later when they learn to read and write. Literacy is rooted in being aware of sounds and being able to discriminate between similar sounds, where they come from and how they are made, with increasing awareness. Phonological awareness 'refers to the ability to hear sounds' (Mallett, 2005: 243).

Looking – sounds of voices come out of mouths

In the first month, babies stare at human faces and are fascinated by them. A newborn baby: 'can be alert to the face of a sympathetic caregiver speaking, drawing comfort from the expression of affection carried by the eyes and the loving voice' (Trevarthen, 2004: 5).

This is an important part of being fed, and babies who are bottle-fed can lose out on this experience unless they are held close like a breastfed baby. Babies (Murray and Andrews, 2000: 8–9) look intently at facial expressions, and the mouth as it moves to talk to the baby. They stick out their tongue if someone does that to them (you have to wait patiently for them to imitate this). They move in response to you, if you say hallo in an excited way, or smile at them, so much so that neuroscientist Colwyn Trevarthen says it is as if they are dancing with you, as you move together, responding to each other's faces. This subtle kind of imitation is an essential aspect of the journey a child takes into literacy.

The baby is gazing at his mother, and she returns the gaze and talks to him. This is important in developing language

Movement – feedback

We also see babies moving their heads so as to follow adult movements, or to track where a brother or sister moves across the room.

For the purposes of this chapter, one of the most exciting aspects of the baby's development in the first month is the way they hold their hands tightly closed, and often tuck their thumbs in under their fingers (Bruce and Meggitt, 2007: 42–3).

They open their hands in order to grasp an adult's finger. One of Tina's most wonderful memories is, when she was 3 years and 6 months old, seeing her baby brother a few hours after his birth, and putting her little finger next to his closed

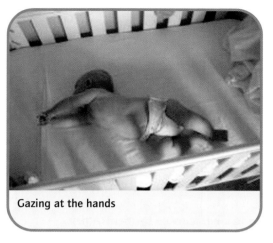

Gazing at the hands

hand. He opened it and grasped her finger. From that moment they bonded and she has deeply loved him ever since.

We begin to see babies watching their hands and playing with their fingers. They might hold something like a rattle for a short time before dropping it. They are beginning to sort out that people make sounds, and so do objects.

In the next months, babies will often play with their toes and feet when they are lying on their backs. This is because the spine is developing strength and they can reach further.

The brain is part of the central nervous system. The other parts of the nervous system are the spinal cord and the peripheral system (which include the sensory nerves for input and motor nerves for acting out what the brain says). The central nervous system has a genetically pro-grammed sequence of development. Put simply, it develops from 'tail to head'. The top of the head, the cerebral cortex region of the brain, develops last. (Meade, 2003: 6)

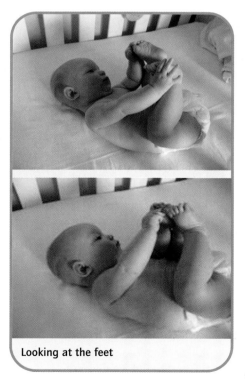

Looking at the feet

Parents and carers interacting with very young children through movement and non-verbal communication in dance-like ways

The work of Colwyn Trevarthen (2004: 3) at Edinburgh University has, across the years, shown that babies in the first three months are able to take part in what he calls 'proto-conversations'. It is as if babies are 'born to find someone who communicates interest and affection'.

Babies are biologically driven to make their families engage with their smiles, coo vocalizations, make hand gestures, and to be able to tell us when they want to socialize through gaze approach, or need a rest from 'chatting' through gaze avoidance.

By the time they can sit, Trevarthen (2004: 2) has found that babies can 'negotiate interests, intentions and feelings' with two other babies at a similar point in their development and learning, without the help of adults. They use imitation as a way of setting up communication. If one baby picks up an object from the treasure basket, the others do the same, and often take them from each other.

Before this, newborn babies 'imitate simple expressions of face, hands or voice, and expect to get a response from the person they are attending to' (Trevarthen, 2004: 3).

Sympathy neurons in the brain

It has become clear that the cells which 'mirroring' effects have been recorded are part of widely distributed systems through the brain, that both move and feel with another subject. It might be better to call these neural mechanisms of *sympathy*, which is the Greek word meaning 'moving and feeling with'. (Trevarthen, 2004: 6)

One of the themes throughout this book is the way that children understand things before they can perform. They can hear the sound 'j' before they can artic- ulate it. Understanding precedes competence. Competence precedes perform- ance. This is so for a baby's ability to understand the mechanics of having a 'conversation' before words are possible.

It is therefore very important for babies and young children to spend time with adults who help them to develop understanding as they see, hear and move.

The baby, aged, fifteen months, sits on his mother's knee inside the Oogly Boogly dome. This is a neutral space and soft music is playing, so that it is not silent. The baby feels secure and bangs his foot on the padded floor. It makes a thudding sound.

The actor, sitting opposite the baby, bangs his foot in the same way, mirroring the baby's action. The baby looks at the actor for a moment, and then lifts his foot and pulls his sock off.

The actor lifts his foot and pulls his sock off. The baby realises the actor is copying him and that whatever he does, the actor will do it. The baby also realises that he is the one in control of the game. (Observation, Spratt, 2006)

The whole focus of the theatre company's 'Oogly Boogly' experience is based on observation. The actors and dancers taking part in the play have spent a long time focusing on how to observe the sounds, postures, facial expressions, eye-pointing, gaze, intonation, tone, rhythm and movement of the babies they work with. The work of the theatre company shows how non-verbal communication between child and actor, sitting safely on their parent's knee to begin with, provides the signal to the adult. The child is on the edge or cusp of spoken language. The 'Oogly Boogly' experience is therefore only for babies typically aged from 12 to 18 months (or chil- dren at a similar point of development) as they are developing:

- a sense of physical self-embodiment
- a sense of themselves as a thinker (meta-cognition)
- a sense of their feelings and management of them (emotional literacy)
- and on the cusp of language.

Judy Dunn (1988) also comments on the way babies delight in their parents and family echoing back what they say and how they move.

Damasio (2004) suggests a 'nesting principle' where the baby is laying down the foundations for communication and later reading and writing.

This links with the work of Roberto Frabetti, who makes theatre for very young children. He suggests:

> Listening is complex – it means paying attention to what is not said, to the hidden, to the evoked ... the children's eyes and silences go hand in hand and sometimes they open doors to hidden worlds. Most of the time we are not able to see them, and then we lose a good chance to be astonished. (Frabetti, 2005: 64)

The silences and pauses of very young children as we interact with them, are important ways in which they build up their understanding and ability to communicate. Children's pauses are: 'Long pauses that make you consider time from a different point of view' (Frabetti, 2005: 70).

Babies have a fine sense of timing and rhythm in conversations

We find, in the first three months:

- syllabic beat
- phrasing
- sympathetic co-ordination of movements, looking and sounds between baby and familiar, loved adult
- call and response
- emphasis and intonation.

The work of Gunilla Preisler at Stockholm University shows that blind babies take part in these proto-conversations too. A mother and her blind 5-month-old daughter share a song:

> Their delicate and subtle duetting is made even more instructive by the fact that this infant was born totally and permanently blind. She has never seen her hands or the hands of any other person. And yet it appears she can accompany portions of the song her mother sings with expressive hand gestures that display intelligent precision and even some anticipation of melody. Over the past months the baby girl has become very familiar with these compositions by Alice Tegnar, whose children's songs are much loved throughout Scandinavia. (Trevarthen, 1999–2000: 186)

Hands and language go together. We naturally use our hands as we speak. Trevarthen suggests that hand movements add emotive meaning to what we say. The two systems, hand gesture and speaking, develop in an integrated way. Sitting on our hands while we speak makes it almost impossible to say what we want to say!

The Papousek parents found their baby daughter, at 4 months, used the parental tones and rhythms: 'A diary of their daughter documented the infant's enjoyment of nursery songs, and her private practice of acquired musical forms' (Trevarthen, 2004: 9).

Daniel Stern notes that the way the parent or carer picks up the baby's expressions is of great importance. This has far-reaching implications for children in group care. The importance of babies in group care having a key person cannot be overemphasized. This is a central part of the *Early Years Foundation Stage*.

Baby songs

Once again, Froebel (1782–1852) shines out as a pioneer educator who realized the importance of singing to babies and involving them in movement play. He did this through his 'Mother Songs', thus raising the status of motherhood at a time when babies were farmed out to be cared for by wet nurses, often with little or no contact with their parents. The recent research we have touched on demonstrates the importance of these early forms of introduction to music and dance through movement, looking at each other and listening. Imitation is key to this. Trevarthen and colleagues have collected what they call 'Baby Songs' in many languages. These resonate with Froebel's 'Mother Songs'.

Trevarthen and colleagues have found that baby songs in the English language have these characteristics:

- The songs are typically four stanzas with four simple phrases.
- There is often a rhyming pattern at the end of the second and fourth lines.

Cheerful baby songs

- The rhythm is often iambic and a dancing rhythm.
- The base pulse is *andante*.
- There are variations in rhythm to give excitement in the last two lines.
- There are simple shifts of pitch.
- It is easy for babies (often only 4 months old) to predict the timing and rhyming features of the song.

For example, a baby might sing on top of the mother's singing exactly on top of the word 'bear' when singing,

> Round and round the garden
> Like a teddy bear
> One step, two step
> Tickly under there

Lullabies to soothe

- The rhythm is often slow (*adagio*) and soothing with a gentle rocking rhythm.
- It is soothing in pitch, without the moments of excitement.

For example, the song might be

> Bye Baby Bunting
> Daddy's gone a-hunting
> Gone to fetch a rabbit skin
> To wrap a Baby Bunting in.

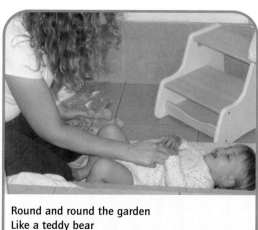

Round and round the garden
Like a teddy bear
One step, two step
Tickly under there

Babies become interested in objects as well as people

At around 3 months a baby's hands begin to open from the tight little fists they have been. They start to grasp and release objects, so we put rattles in their hands. But this interest in objects comes long after engagement with people, as we have so far explored in this chapter. 'Objects are now discovered at an accelerating pace, by the combined application of hands, eyes, ears and mouth to pick up useful information' (Trevarthen, 2004: 14).

From the beginning, we hang mobiles above the cradle for babies to look at. Penny Greenland (2006) points out that, as children develop and need to try out stretching, they need mobiles they can reach for, and objects they can hold with the arm extended. It is the same with the toes. We often see babies stretching their leg to kick a toy in the cradle. They are on their back, but the satisfaction registers on their face as their foot makes contact and they feel the connection.

Hayden, because he is mobile, can select the objects he wants. He pushes away the second soft ball and keeps the other one. The soft ball is a favourite, and this is typical of crawling babies. He knows he can make the ball roll away from him, and he likes to watch this. It is exercising, quite naturally, his developing ability to track a moving object in a trajectory. Later he will need his tracking ability to follow a line of print in a text.

Parents/key persons beginning the movement play

Trevarthen and colleagues show that after the first three months parents tend to engage their babies in movement play with stronger forces and rhythms, sharing the drama, excitement and laughter. 'Soon play routines are discovered that facilitate lively and enthusiastic participation and make the baby laugh when half-expected surprises occur, or when the baby knows they are coming' (Trevarthen, 2004: 14). Later this will turn into the rough and tumble play which Penny Greenland (2006) emphasizes at the toddler stage of development, when children are coming into walking, talking and pretending.

Before children are mobile, the baby songs have an important place. The adult tickles the child, and initiates movement accompanied by song. In this chapter, we have seen this in the rhythm, 'Round and round the garden like a teddy bear'. This means that looking, listening and moving are co-ordinating in the service of communication and language development. This develops into finger rhymes. The importance of the hand therefore continues with refinement of the use of the fingers.

The adult engages the baby in songs

This little piggy went to market

This little piggy stayed at home
This little piggy ate roast beef
This little piggy had none

This little piggy went
Wee wee wee
All the way home.

Sharing jokes and laughter

These are important in the baby songs and tickling games. Bateson (1956) showed that as well as jokes and laughter, grammatical rules, poetic and dramatic forms with narrative plots as well as rules of music and dance also nest in baby songs. During all this fun and laughter, babies are communicating about communicating, which is called 'meta-communication'.

The grammatical forms include:

- entailment
- qualification
- contrast
- repetition with changed emphasis
- subordination
- opposition
- release.

Hands as objects

In an earlier section in this chapter, we looked at the importance of objects for babies. But we need to be careful here.

> In a modern home there are electronic toys that are programmed to play tunes or carry out spontaneous simulations of human or animal action. Such 'robots' are exciting, indeed – but we have to wonder if they threaten to eliminate interaction such as a baby can only have with a live mind in a live body. (Trevarthen, 2004: 15–16)

Froebel's understanding of the importance of 'Mother Songs', which Trevarthen and colleagues write about as 'Baby Songs' make a major contribution to the developing learning of babies about communication and language, in which later literacy nests.

Pat-a-cake, pat-a-cake

Baker's man
Bake me a cake
As fast as you can
Pat it and prick it
And mark it with 'B'
Put it in the oven for baby and me
Baby and me, baby and me
Put it in the oven
For baby and me.

IN SUMMARY

The parent or key person encourages the use of the hands in this song. This lays the way for finger rhymes, which are explored in the next chapter:

- the importance of the baby's relationship with warm affectionate parents, siblings and key people
- how we can be helpful to children in developing communication and language from the moment a baby is born because the baby has a need to learn by picking up ideas from a community of people they love
- how babies use imitation and mirroring to co-ordinate the integrated strands of movements, looking and listening
- how early we see babies showing an intention to communicate with us, and an ability to engage in proto-conversations, because this is how they begin to learn what other people know and do
- how music and dance are there from the beginning, and how they support the essentials of later literacy, such as rhythm, rhyme, intonation and alliteration.

Chapter 4

Finger Rhymes

To work with and not against nature:

- parents and key people are of central importance
- by the time a baby is sitting, a great deal has been going on with the baby's developing vision, proprioception (feeling where their body is located with reference to the floor) and balance (the midline) so that they operate together
- the hands continue to play an important part in the developing learning.

Sitting – fingers and thumbs

Tiny babies knead and grip as they feed, using a palmar grip. The movement encourages sucking. This link between the mouth and the hand is called the Babkin response. Being able to grip is important. But so is learning how to let go of objects at will. When sitting babies drop toys over the edge of the high chair, that is exactly what they are doing! This will be important for pencil control later on.

The palmar grasp is followed by the pincer grasp. And they use their index finger and thumb in opposition to transfer a toy from one hand to the other, and they put objects in their mouths. Sally Goddard-Blythe (2004: 52) stresses the importance of the development of co-ordinations between hand and mouth. She says they are 'cortical maps' for the brain. Some babies seem to blink as they suck, especially premature babies. There is a connection between what the baby sees, sucking the hand that brings an object to the mouth, and speech articulation.

The baby who is able to sit unaided will experiment with reaching for objects in front of them, behind them and on the opposite side to the hand with which they reach. There is plenty of toppling over as they work out how to balance around their midline. But this does not put the baby off. Penny Greenland (2006: 163–4), who is Director of the Developmental Movement Centre, says that, fortunately, babies are biologically driven to 'seek out, and create, the experiences they need'. She goes on to say, 'It is active involvement and exploration through movement play that enables a child to become a more mature, efficient organiser of sensory information – providing the foundations for all future learning'.

Crawling – balancing and travelling at the same time

Children need to spend plenty of time on the floor. Penny Greenland (2006) suggests that:

- being on the back and tummy helps children to sense their bodies as they kick their feet and move their hands
- sitting is important. Being able to sit so that you don't topple, and managing to stay that way when you reach around you for objects!
- crawling is important for future learning because it 'supports a strong sense of the centre of the body whilst in motion' (Greenland, 2006). It is the first time that children experience balancing and travelling at the same time
- it is the first time that children look from side to side without moving their head from side to side as they travel along. This will be important in later reading.

Looking ahead and from side to side without moving the head, while travelling along

Sitting and crawling are part of the journey from being curled up in the womb, like a letter 'C' says Penny Greenland (2006), to being in the 'S' shape of the spine standing up.

As children develop, some doors shut as others open. Sarah-Jayne Blakemore and Uta Frith (2005: 31) explain, 'New learning means opening and setting neural connections for important events and closing others that are no longer important and would only be distracting and confusing.'

Babies need to spend time sitting on the floor and crawling so that the closing down of some movements can occur naturally, and in the process open the way for others. If they do not fade, the child could later experience difficulty in sitting still at a table or on a chair.

Building on natural development

During our work together, Jenny led the group in a piece of professional development work emphasizing that finger rhymes are more important than we had known previously. That is why we are devoting a whole chapter to this aspect of learning.

Babies, sitters, crawlers and wobbly walkers are learning things which will be important to them later on. Sally Goddard-Blythe (2004: 65) says, 'reflex movements in nerve cells lie at the root of every act of higher will: the highest acts of will merely have deliberation, choice, and inhibition added to these foundation reflexes'. Neuroscientist, Antonio Damasio (2004), says the same thing in a different way. He says a child's development

> consists of having parts of simpler reactions incorporated as components of more elaborate ones, a nesting principle of the simple within the complex ... Each of the different regulatory reactions is not a radically different process, built from scratch for a specific purpose. Rather, each reaction consists of tinkered rearrangements of bits and parts of the simpler processes below. They are all aimed at the same overall goal – survival with well-being – but each of the tinkered rearrangements is secondarily aimed at a new problem whose solution is necessary for the overall goal to be achieved. (Damasio, 2004: 37–8)

Put simply, this means:

- babies and toddlers who get appropriate support there and then, are also being helped in their future learning
- we need to know the key aspects of a child's development in communication, relationships, language, play and movement
- we need to know what is involved in the subject knowledge of reading and writing (literacy), literature and information.

The best image to capture this is of a tree: 'a tall messy tree with progressively higher and more elaborate branches coming off the main trunks and thus maintaining a two-way communication with the roots. The history of evolution is written all over that tree' (Damasio, 2004: 38).

Penny Greenland and Sally Goddard-Blythe point out that most children pass through these sequences of development with ease, naturally playing and becoming walkers with all the important building blocks in place. It is therefore important to stress, as the English *Early Years Foundation Stage* Framework (DfES, 2007a) does, that we need to create environments that are enabling, that positive relationships are crucial, that we need to know how children develop and learn, and how to help them do so, and that each child is a unique child. Playing at being a dog, and crawling as part of that, making a den under the table, all contribute to the ability to use the hands and fingers to the full. When a child crawls, two important things happen to the hand:

- The hand is spread out.
- Leaning on the floor puts pressure on the palm of the hand, which the child feels – a feedback.

How finger rhymes build on natural development

Finger rhymes co-ordinate hand and mouth movements, looking, remembering, rhythm, and match sight with sound. They extend the learning of the last chapter. All these are important in developing the essentials of literacy and a love of literature, and in seeking knowledge and information.

Singing at the same time as the finger movements in co-ordination is a huge challenge for young children. The concentration is deep

Trying to 'do my ruby ring'

Matching sight and sounds

The ability to match sounds and sights takes years to develop, but it is very important in learning to read and write. Finger rhymes help the process along in ways which are right for toddlers and young children.

When babies hear a sound, they often freeze and listen. They are waiting to find out if it brings comfort or danger. When they hear an unfamiliar sound they also open their eyes wide in a startle response and then look from place to place to try and see the source of the sound. Then they fix their eyes on it.

Finger songs and rhymes link sound, sight and movement

This helps toddlers and young children to co-ordinate sound, sight and movement which in turn helps children towards future reading and writing.

Three-year-old Ben said to his key person, 'I can do my ruby ring now.' He held up his finger to show her, and started to sing, with his hands behind his back, 'Ruby ring, ruby ring, where are you?' and then brought out his hands in front, raised his fourth fingers and sang, 'Here I am, Here I am, How do you do?' He is linking the appropriate finger, the movement and the words of the song.

How it looks

Another child, also 3 years old, often wears his Spiderman outfit to the setting. He has also learnt the Tommy Thumb finger rhyme. One day he sang his key person a song he had created himself, based on this. He put his hand behind his back, and sang, Spiderman, Spiderman, where are you?' He brought his hands out in front of him and put his fingers into a shape where he clenched the hand, but put his second and third finger out on each hand. He thrust the hand forward in time to the rhythm and sang, 'Here I am, Here I am, How do you do?'

This is a variation on a theme, which is a strategy through which creativity often presents itself (Bruce, 2004a: 97).

Sorting out sounds – phonological awareness

When we sing, we extend the vowel sounds, and this helps the phonological awareness which will be crucial in learning to read later on.

> Tooooooooooommy Thuuuuuuumb, Tooooooooommy Thuuuuuumb
> Wheeeeeeere aaaaaaare yoooooooou?
> Heeeeeeere I am, Heeeeeere I am,
> Hooooooow do you dooooooo?

Tomatis (in Goddard-Blythe, 2004) says that using the voice in singing helps children (including children with hearing impairments) to develop their listening skills. Children need to be able to distinguish between the different sounds of the language. Adam Ockelford (1996) has developed songs about everyday situations, such as greetings, partings and meals to help children with visual and complex needs communicate. Singing 'It's dinner time' often brings a response, when simply saying it does not.

Finger rhymes help children to develop the rhythm of language

Hearing words in a song helps children to develop an understanding of rhythms and syllabification, which is crucial in later reading. Rhythm is a sequence of movements in time.

> Toh mmee Thumb.

It is easy to sense that Tommy has two syllables and Thumb only has one. This does not have to be discussed with a young child, but they feel it through the rhythm of the finger rhyme.

Finger rhymes give children memory aids which help language to develop

Finger rhymes help children to develop their memory, which is important in learning a sight vocabulary in later reading.

Finger rhymes help the relationship between the young child and the parent, older sibling or key person

The *Early Years Foundation Stage* says in the commitment adults need to have to **supporting learning** in young children:

> Warm, trusting relationships with knowledgeable adults support children's learning more effectively than any amount of resources. (DfES, 2007a: 2:3)

The relationships children have with people they spend time with are of fundamental importance.

Children do not develop good language unless they are spoken to in an atmosphere of warmth and affection. Communication is about looking at each other, and engaging with each other. The development of language is fostered in the use of finger rhymes, because children are looking at the adult in order to imitate the finger movements and singing them too once they get the movements under control. Singing and moving together is a time-honoured way of enjoying being together. It encourages integration of movement, sound and vision in the brain.

Finger rhymes help the development of muscles in young children, which in turn aid later writing skills

Children love the challenge of trying to place their fingers correctly in the finger rhymes. Because they are actively moving as they do this, they have a multi-sensory experience which helps them to learn about the shape of letters and how to make them later on. This gives them direct feedback through their own body in a way that other experiences do not. This is why it is so powerful.

Enjoying the challenge, and feeling part of a group that is supportive and wanting everyone to succeed

Finger rhymes help children to track detail, important when reading print later

They see the fingers changing from one shape to another. Ben has worked out that he can vary the shapes and make his own, changing the one finger of the 'Tommy Thumb' rhyme into the two-fingered shape of his own composition of the 'Spiderman' song.

Marie Clay (1982) reminds us that young children scan around words on a page, rather than fixing on one word. It is important in reading to track and then converge the gaze and fix it on the word to be read. Having a fine focus on the finger and tracking it to then fix it into a shape helps this process along.

Finger rhymes are important for children with learning difficulties and disabilities

- A child with a **learning difficulty** needs plenty of time to learn a finger rhyme, but with repetition this is achieved. Children should not be rushed through their learning.

- A child with a **visual impairment** can be taught the actions, and will often readily learn the words and tune. It is of great benefit to children if they can develop a strong sense of their own body and how it moves and feels. It is what Penny Greenland calls the 'felt sense of living'.
- A child with a **hearing impairment** greatly appreciates the actions with the fingers. It helps them with a sense of pattern and sequence which will later help them to read.

Introducing finger rhymes to children

Jenny Spratt explored finger rhymes as part of her studies (Froebel Diploma, accredited by Roehampton University for the National Froebel Foundation). She became aware of the mother songs and finger rhymes devised in the mid-nineteenth century by Friedrich Froebel. Blakemore and Frith point out (2005: 128) 'research suggests that the brain assigns a quantity of synapses to the processing of the fingers in accordance with how much the fingers are used'.

What Jenny was finding out about finger rhymes seemed so important that we gave them a much greater place. In fact, we realized, we had neglected them, either by lumping them together with action songs and not making a distinction between finger rhymes and action songs, or by encouraging the use of finger puppets and hand puppets as props for songs and stories.

An important Froebelian principle is to introduce the whole before isolating the parts of a finger rhyme. Jenny therefore suggested that it might be helpful to introduce the finger rhymes to children in three stages.

Stage 1

Introduce rhymes that just use the hand so that children get used to the concept of unity (Froebel) within the whole. The rhymes should involve the whole hand and all 10 fingers, opening and shutting.

Stage 2

Introduce rhymes that use the fingers to represent parts of the body, again supporting the child's concept of unity (Froebel). The fingers are part of the hand, which is part of the body. Different fingers are isolated during the finger rhyme.

Stage 3

Introduce rhymes that use the fingers to represent objects from nature, community, food, and so on.

Finger dexterity as emergent 'writing'

Finger rhymes enhance the child's possibility to 'write' for themselves, improving the **dexterity of their fingers** and hand control, whereas the poetry card aids their ability to recognize printed words. The **opening up** and **extending of the palm** of the hand are important in this. Since many children are not, in modern life, spending time on the floor, or crawling, this aspect of development is becoming neglected.

Through Jenny's work in this area, we have become aware, when visiting different children in a range of settings and situations, that many young children seem to be sitting and moving about with clenched hands. This could be for various reasons. Here is one reason, first expressed by Elizabeth Harrison in 1895: 'The clenched hands denote the struggle within, and great artists often use them as the only marked sign of the inward turmoil which the calm face and strong will are determined to conceal. The open and extended palm indicates entire freedom from deceit or concealment' (Harrison, 1895: 166).

Spreading the hand out, and feeling feedback from the pressure of the fingers in a fist on the palm of the hand are important for later development of writing

Note the clenching and opening out of the hands

Finger rhymes should not be used in isolation from other types of rhyme

Finger rhymes are part of a range of rhyme, from finger rhymes to action songs, nursery rhymes, poetry cards and books of stories and information. The children need to experience the gross motor movements and the music, singing, use of three-dimensional objects, the rhythm and rhyme to help them be able to fine focus on the fingers.

The photographs in this chapter are from observations taken at a nursery school in which children aged from 2 to 5 years are with a nursery teacher. The children are from different community and cultural groups, with some children having an identified special need/disability as the intake for the nursery school is from across the city, depending upon parental choice and availability.

The teacher, having attended the training session, decided to use the proposed three stages of finger rhymes and was amazed at what she found.

It is interesting that one of the rhymes the children enjoyed is 'The Beehive', which was created by Emile Poulsson in 1893, based on the format of Froebel's finger plays, for one of the early kindergartens in the USA.

Stage 1

The important thing when selecting finger rhymes for this stage is that they should involve the whole hand and all 10 fingers, opening and shutting. These were particularly popular and much loved by the children. It is important to have a set of core finger rhymes to share together so that the children become proficient in them as they are regularly repeated in a sustained way. These are just examples:

Open, Shut Them

Open, shut them, Open, shut them,
Give a little clap.
Open, shut them, Open, shut them
Put them on your lap.

Creep them, creep them, creep them, creep them,
Right up to your chin, chin, chin,
Open wide your little mouth
(*Hesitate*)
But do not put them in.

Sitting on the floor is important

It is important for the children to sit on the floor, so that they are 'grounded'. This links with the work in developmental movement practice (Jabadao) of Penny Greenland and her colleagues. As we have seen earlier in the chapter, connection with the floor is important as a reference point for the body. It is very hard to keep the midline and balance for a young child if they have to sit on a chair.

Sing the finger rhyme very slowly

Children are trying to focus on the detail, and they need you to do the rhyme slowly so that they can work it out. It is rather like learning a foreign language. It helps if people speak slowly.

The children enjoyed these songs and found them easier than the next stage, when they had to isolate different fingers. It helped to talk about what was happening, such as asking them to squeeze their hands to look like a ball, and keep them still, and then lift one finger at a time. In other words, language (as Vygotsky, 1978, suggests) supported the way the children understood and were able to carry out the mechanics of the actions.

When concentrating hard and doing something very difficult, it is important not to rush children

Ten Little Fingers

I have ten little fingers,
They all belong to me.
I can make them do things.
Would you like to see?
I can shut them up tight,
Open them wide.
I can put them together,
Or make them hide.
I can make them jump high,
Or make them go low.
I can fold them up quietly (fold arms)
And sit just so.

What were the results (outcomes) for stage 1 finger rhymes?

- The children were extending the palms of their hands more often in a variety of situations. Their hands were not so often clenched. Hands were more flexible.
- Children were helped to be more aware of the different sensations in their hands, when stretching and squeezing.
- The visual gaze at their hands was enhanced.
- Getting to know themselves as physical beings was encouraged, (what Penny Greenland calls the 'felt sense of living').
- Children enjoyed the sense of anticipation.

The teacher picked out the children's pleasure in anticipation as a key element in introducing finger rhymes at this early stage: 'The children feel a sense of anticipation for the word, waiting for their favourite word to come.'

Stage 2

Go from whole hand to fingers

The important thing during this stage is to help children to isolate the different fingers during the finger rhyme, and help them to name each finger. Choose finger rhymes with this in mind.

In stage 2, children have to isolate each finger, so this song is a bit more challenging than 'Ten Little Fingers' or 'Open, Shut Them', in stage 1.

Tommy Thumb

Tommy thumb, Tommy thumb,
Where are you?
Here I am, Here I am, How do you do?

Peter pointer, Peter pointer
Where are you?
Here I am, Here I am, How do you do?

Toby tall, Toby tall
Where are you?
Here I am, Here I am, How do you do?

Ruby ring, Ruby ring
Where are you?
Here I am, Here I am, How do you do?

Baby small, Baby small
Where are you?
Here I am, Here I am, How do you do?

Fingers all, Fingers all,
Where are you?
Here we are, Here we are, How do you do?

Sitting on the floor is still important

So is singing the finger rhyme slowly

Talk about the position of the fingers

Moving and talking about what and how you are moving helps the child to succeed.

Encourage children to look at both hands by doing so yourself as you sing

This kind of tracking is very important in later reading. When babies crawl they are looking from side to side of their midline while they are travelling, without moving their head, which is an important development. Later, when children read, they are tracking the line of print with their eyes, without moving their head from side to side.

Encourage children to watch their fingers

Children find it fascinating to change their fingers in position. They like to have names for them, such as thumb, pointing finger, little finger, and so on.

Encourage children to use their fingers as symbols

Walking, talking and pretending are important developments during the first three years. A symbol is something which stands for something else. An excellent way for young children to explore symbols is to let them see and understand that their own fingers can by made to stand for something else.

What were the results (outcomes) for stage 2 finger rhymes?

- The teacher found that the children developed better control of their fingers (and so did the staff and parents!).
- Visual tracking improved.
- There was an increase in vocabulary.
- Children anticipated the words and finger movements.
- Although adults focused on naming the fingers, the children began to see that they could use their fingers as symbols to represent characters in a story, which prepared them for stage 3.

The teacher felt that it was at stage 2 that she saw most difference, although all three stages are important. From the point of view of **physical development** and **movement** encouraged through finger rhymes, she found that, as in stage 1:

Both boys and girls enjoy finger rhymes. They help all children to engage in an experience which sets them on a good journey into literacy

sitting on the floor helped children to be comfortable, grounded and balanced. This enables them to move the top part of their bodies with the bottom part feeing safe and secure. The children become aware of themselves and of their physicality, but have time to look and listen. It is the physical skill to focus close on the fingers and then be able to focus beyond, as the hand is held up.

Although these are deeply important aspects of learning, perhaps the most exciting is the way that children responded to the 'literature' elements involved. She says: 'It is the 'pantomime' – the senses are there in the background, which allows the child to develop his individual style, leading into free-flow play (Bruce, 1991). For boys the finger rhymes have led them to being interested in key stories.'

The links with **music** are also strong. The sound elements are crucial to learning to read later. 'It is the longer rhymes that children enjoy the most. They enjoy linking sound rhythm and beat to the phonic, but most of all they enjoy the anticipation and variety.'

The children also developed a sense of **drama**. 'The children change the identity of the fingers and their voices to represent the different fingers. They can be what they want them to be.'

The teacher felt that a key feature of the finger rhymes was that of touch, which children do not experience when using finger puppets.

It is the sense of touch in the different movements, supported by the looking that is important. The children refer to 'Ruby Ring' as the 'tricky one', but they can now hold 'Ruby Ring' up straight. They will often talk about what 'Ruby Ring' is doing while they are engaged in other activities, and practitioners will also ask the children, 'Can you see how your "Peter pointer" is painting? Does it feel different with "Ruby ring" or "Baby small"? Is the sensation different?' The identity of 'Ruby ring' is big!

So, although stage 2 is about isolating the fingers and naming them, the children quickly grasped the potential of using their separate fingers as symbols. They readily turned them into characters, and short narratives and storylines were soon developing around them. It is almost impossible to keep children in stage 2 from stage 3. Only the adults need to keep them separate in their heads, to ensure children have a balance of each.

Stage 3

The finger rhymes help the whole body control, and vice versa

It is important not to introduce finger rhymes in isolation from action songs. They help each other, so children need both.

Gross motor movements are crucial in development and learning

The action songs in stage 3 link gross motor with the fine motor finger rhymes, and act as a bridge between them. The hands are extended into larger movements of the arm. The gaze is also extended further from the body to look at the hand from a greater distance.

In later literacy development, children will need to have both good gross motor and fine motor skills. The gross shoulder movement controls the fine motor movements of the fingers, as anyone who has broken a shoulder and tried to write to a friend will know!

Characters and stories using the fingers as symbols: nature, people and objects

We have based our collection of finger rhymes on the classification of Friedrich Froebel in his 'Mother Songs', using the categories nature, people and objects.

This is a finger rhyme about nature:

Two Little Dicky Birds

Two little dicky birds, sitting on a wall
One called Peter, one called Paul.
Fly away Peter, fly away Paul
Come back Peter, come back Paul.

This is a finger rhyme about people:

Two Fat Gentlemen

Two fat gentlemen met in the lane,
Bowed most politely, bowed once again.
How do you do? How do you do?
How do you do again?

Two thin ladies met in the lane,
Bowed most politely, bowed once again.
How do you do? How do you do?
How do you do again?

Two tall policemen met in the lane,
Bowed most politely, bowed once again.
How do you do? How do you do?
How do you do again?

Two little schoolboys met in the lane,
Bowed most politely, bowed once again.
How do you do? How do you do?
How do you do again?

Two little babies met in the lane,
Bowed ...

The staff have been impressed at the way the children enjoyed the longer rhymes. They liked the repetition and entered into the spirit of performing the song together.

The last category of finger rhymes involves objects:

The Beehive

Modern version:

Here is the beehive,
But where are the bees?
Hidden away
Where nobody sees.
Look and you'll see them,
Come out of the hive,
One, two, three, four, five
BZZZZZZZZZZZZZZZZZZ

Emilie Poulsson (an early Froebelian) – original version:

Here is the beehive.
Where are the bees?
Hidden away where nobody sees.
Soon they'll come creeping out of the hive –
One! – two! – three! – four! – five!

What are the results (outcomes) of stage 3 finger rhymes?

- Gross and fine motor skills are linked.
- The gaze is extended.

- Characters and stories develop in simple, engaging ways.
- There was symbolic representation.
- Imagination developed (remember the example of the Spiderman finger rhyme created by 3 year old boy?).
- They began to link the finger rhymes to stories.
- They developed a sense of pantomime and drama.

The teacher found that stage 3 focused on gross motor skills using the hands and fingers alongside the rest of the body in controlled movements. We began to realize that covering fingers with finger puppets undermined the learning, rather in the way that in the last chapter Trevarthen suggests that electronic toys, rather than play with a traditional soft ball, undermine the interactions between baby and parent or key person. The noises the toys make and the flashing lights, or the coverings of the fingers by the puppets, are what Bruner calls, 'noisy cues' which are taking children away from the essentials of literacy. The teacher notes:

> The children enjoy the finger rhymes without the puppets just as much.

This teacher who, with her colleagues, decided to explore finger rhymes as a result of the course she attended, said, 'It is stage 3 in the finger rhymes that "grabs" practitioners, but it is probably the least important. Stage 2 is the most important, and stage 1 is very necessary – it is an integral part of development at an early stage. It is finding out about the body – getting to know yourself as a physical being and that your finger looks the same here or there. It is a stage for exploring the senses. The body is feeling really comfortable – the children sit on the floor, so are 'grounded' and this could be anywhere – indoors or outdoors.

IN SUMMARY

In this chapter, we have looked at the important beginnings of multi-sensory learning on the journey into communication, language and literacy:

- how the hands help adults and children to make meaning together through emotive gestures right from the start
- finger rhymes encourage parents and key persons to enjoy early literacy experiences with their children
- the songs using the hands develop the midline, tracking and focus, and co-ordination of hand and eye in physical development, crucial for later literacy
- they help children with fine motor skills and gross motor skills so that each helps the other along in ways which support the development of writing
- finger rhymes are examples of early and engaging opportunities for the development of symbol making and symbol use by children just beginning to represent as they learn to walk, talk and pretend.

Chapter 5

Mark-Making and Writing

Reading and writing are not separate processes. They feed into and off each other. They depend upon each other and they help each other along.

In the previous chapter, we saw how essential to reading and writing it is to have the body co-ordinating in ways which help the physical mechanics of reading and writing. The phonology (sounds and tune of the language) connects with hearing. The sounds link with the movements of the hands and the whole body. Children begin to work out that sounds can be written down as they mark-make, using pencils, paint, and so on. They learn that to do this they need to use symbols which everyone can understand.

Mark-making

The marks children make, their first scribble drawings, are the beginnings of the essentials they need in order to write.

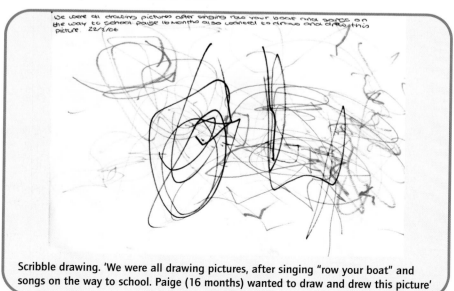

Scribble drawing. 'We were all drawing pictures, after singing "row your boat" and songs on the way to school. Paige (16 months) wanted to draw and drew this picture'

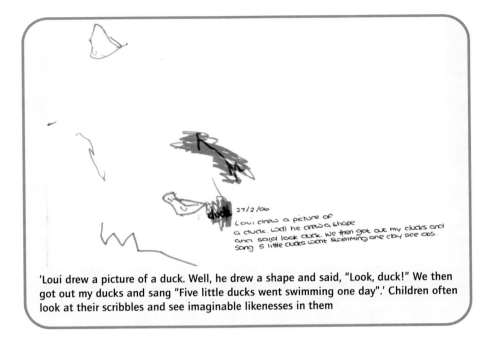

27/2/06
Loui drew a picture of
a duck. Well he drew a shape
and said look duck. We then got out my ducks and
song 5 little ducks went swimming one day see obs.

'Loui drew a picture of a duck. Well, he drew a shape and said, "Look, duck!" We then got out my ducks and sang "Five little ducks went swimming one day".' Children often look at their scribbles and see imaginable likenesses in them

The childminder reports that:

Each time a duck swam away, I hid it under my skirt. Loui loved this and said, 'Where duck gone?' I showed him it was under my skirt. Loui liked this idea and when the next duck swam away he hid it up his trouser leg. Lizzie did the same with her duck, and the last duck she hid up her top. We all laughed as this was very funny. We managed to get all the ducks back out for the last part of the song when all the ducks return.

Lizzie was able to sing the bits of the song I missed out, e.g. I sang 'five little ducks went ... ' And Lizzie would sing 'swimming one day over the hills and far away.' I sang, 'Mother duck said ... ' and again Lizzie would sing 'Quack. Quack, quack, quack' and we all joined in with the 4 little ducks came swimming back. I wrote the words of the song in front of the children and Loui said, 'Julie you writing.' I answered, 'Yes, I am writing'.

Once I had finished writing the words, Lizzie followed them with her finger across the page from left to right as she sang the whole song by herself. Loui also has a go at following the words with his finger and he moved his finger in a circle motion over the words as Lizzie and I sang the words of the song.

Here we see, using play props, rehearsal for segmenting and blending (separate ducks, or ducks altogether on the pond). We see an understanding from Lizzie that print represents meaning, and the glimmerings of this in Paige. The children are seeing what they sing can be written down, and Lizzie has the understanding that it is possible to read back what you have just written down. Reading and writing cannot be separated. What we encode, we decode.

Paige is discovering mark-making. Loui and Lizzie are beginning to see and understand that they can be symbol makers. They can do this through painting or drawing.

The important thing in stage 1 nursery ryhmes is to enjoy them with children, and to act them out, and to leave play props and small world, and books so that they can revisit and try them out in their own time as they wish (Chapter 2). Rhymes build on what is natural to children, and so we, as adults, need to use them in ways which enhance this

Personal symbols are a bridge to shared, conventional symbols

Vygotsky, in the1930s, identified the way that children's drawings develop. Early letters appear in them, and are gradually pushed out to the edge, to become emergent writing.

Children begin to give meaning to what they 'write' and to realize that there is a relationship between how letters and words sound and look. The child is beginning to establish that print represents meaning in books, and that you can actually make your own print! Marie Clay wrote a very important book in 1975, called, *What Did I Write?* Realizing that someone else can read what you have written is one of the most exciting moments in a child's life.

There are layers in this understanding:

- Layer 1 – The toy ducks are objects which carry the meanings around the experiences the children have had of seeing them in the park, and singing the song with Julie.
- Layer 2 – The drawing of the duck was not intentional, but having scribbled, Loui thinks it reminds him of the duck. It is an imagal likeness of a duck.
- Layer 3 – Loui will begin intentionally to draw a duck.
- Layer 4 – Loui will write marks of his own as 'writing' the word 'duck'.
- Layer 5 – Louis will begin to use conventional letters to make the word 'duck'.

Piaget helps us to value the personal symbols children make. They are the bridge between:

- objects holding meaning (the toy duck as part of the much loved song, and the drawing of the duck Loui has made)
- symbols. The child makes marks on paper. Loui did not set out to draw a duck, but the marks he has made become a personal symbol, holding meaning for him.

Bialystok (1991: 78) says objects (like the toy ducks the children use in the song) are imbued with meaning for that child. Loui's drawing is also an object full of meaning for him.

But, the letters of the alphabet are not full of meaning for him, except the letters of his own name. The alphabet letters are not personal objects. They are shared symbols representing shared meaning. This means they do not hold personal meanings.

When he is 4 years old, Loui's mother suggests he might write a 'thank you' card for Julie, and goes to find one. While she is gone, he writes on a piece of paper, 'J'. After a pause, he adds, 'uli'. He has written 'Julie'. His mother is thrilled. He says it is like his name (which has the letters 'u', 'l' and 'i'). He has understood that letters are symbols which represent meanings (Julie's name).

Amanda began to write the 'A' for Amanda. Her family were thrilled. A few weeks later she started to write the letter on its side. When asked why, she replied, 'I've fallen over'. The letter is still a personal object for her, and does not yet represent shared meaning.

Conversations are between people. They are immediate and full of thoughts and feelings. We often do not meet the people who write to us or write books

It is very important to understand, as Margaret Donaldson (1978: 178) reminds us, that writing is often remote. We see the person reading to us, talking to us, writing a shopping list or an invitation, or we find out information for ourselves. But the person who wrote a book or poem is more often than not unknown to us.

This is why shopping lists, messages and greetings cards, written in the presence of the child are important everyday situations where children see people writing, and realize that what we say, think and feel can be written down.

The importance of your name

The child's name is usually the first fixed string of letters to be written spontaneously as a word. This is because of the emotional element. The name is part of a child's identity.

However, we need a note of caution here. Children are able to respond to being called different names in different contexts with different people. There are cultural variations in this too. Often, children have formal names and family names.

Margaret Donaldson points out that when our learning makes human sense to us, we are able to tackle some quite abstract ideas. She says that one way in which learning becomes meaningless is to put children in a context-free situation. They will then import their own ideas in order to create meaning, based on what makes human sense.

To read and write: 'It is necessary to become skilled in manipulating systems and in abstracting forms and patterns' (Donaldson, in ECP, 2005: 18). She points out that things like engineering depend on being able to function in a real world with the support of familiar events: 'disembedded thinking, although by definition it calls for the ability to stand back from life, yields its greatest riches when it is conjoined with doing' (Donaldson, in ECP, 2005: 18).

Children are natural problem-solvers and problem-generators (Karmiloff-Smith, 1992), because they are human. The brain embraces problem-solving. There is now a wealth of research literature showing the way that children tease out how to write down the words they hear. (Bissex, 1980; Ferreiro, 1997). The

Lizzie's name

Basic Skills Agency have written a modern-day summary building on the edifice of research and presenting this in an accessible way to share with parents (Basic Skills Agency, 2005).

In order to write, children need:

- to work out the phoneme/grapheme links (to link sounds and letters)
- to be able to segment and blend, blend and segment
- to begin to see that these are placed in words
- to see how words are placed in sentences.

But this does not mean that children can not write, or have a go at writing, until all of these things are in place. Writing is one of those marvellous areas of development and learning where you find out and understand as you go. Children writing in the English language need this natural problem-solving approach to writing, which is fortunately part of human brain function, more than children writing in other languages. This is because English is one of the most irregular languages in the world.

English is one of the most irregular languages in the world

George has to learn that although his name sounds as if it starts with a J, in fact it starts with a G. What sound can you hear at the start of **Shannon**? **Sian**? **Sean**? **Charlotte**? The sounds are the same, but the written forms are different. As Richard Feynman (1990), the Nobel Prize-winning physicist, said, 'The thing that doesn't fit is the most interesting.'

Lucy spontaneously copied the words of the poem onto four pages. She then added 'by Lucy' independently on the front cover

Children and adults use what they know to find out what they don't know

Lucy is 4 years old and is at her pre-school playgroup. She wanted to write out the poetry card, 'To market, to market to buy a fat pig'.

There are several important things here:

- She uses what she knows to write independently. She has learnt to write 'by' through all the drawings and paintings she has labelled as her own. According to *Letters and Sounds* (DfES, 2007b: 15) research shows 'even when words are recognised apparently at sight, this recognition is the most efficient when it is underpinned by grapheme-phoneme knowledge'.
- We recognize irregular, 'tricky' (DfES, 2007b: 48) words more easily when they have emotional meaning for us. Our names do. So do words like 'love'. As Marian Whitehead points out, it is difficult to fall in love with words like 'to', 'the' or 'go'. But the word 'no' might well have more meaning. It is bathed in emotion and personal meanings!
- Lucy can write her own name independently. This is a huge boost to her well-being. Finding she can write even a small part of what she wanted to say encouraged her to keep going, and believe in herself as a writer.
- The leading teacher discusses Lucy's writing with the practitioners in the pre-school and the leader of the early years pedagogy team. They agree that Lucy 'understands the purpose of print as well as an appreciation of how books work. Her letter formation is accurate and clear and she is beginning to space each word appropriately'.

Adults who set copying tasks for children are not helpful

Dreary exercises in copying are a waste of time and are demoralizing. Tracing words is even less helpful, and gives the message, you cannot do this, so you had better trace the letters.

But many children want to copy quite naturally. Lucy cannot say this, but she is trying to feel the flow of the words and capture the syntax. She is beginning to understand that writing is made up of flow and sentences. The syntax is the order of the words as they are spoken, and then keeping the same order as the words are written down. (Mallett, 2005)

Writing her name, which she does not need to copy, Lucy has got a small fixed string of letters and made them into a word. She managed that on her own. She has needed to learn this as sight vocabulary, as the phoneme-grapheme link in L-u-cy is not obvious. But this is so with much of the English language.

Copying the poetry card, she is taking on the challenge of a much longer fixed string – the sentences making up the words of the rhyme. In this way, she is beginning to sort out letters, words and sentences, although she does not know it yet, and cannot talk about it. Understanding comes before competence and performance in writing, and every aspect of learning.

It helps to look at drawings and writing together

The group of practitioners looking at Lucy's drawing and writing will share what they are thinking with Lucy's parents. They are impressed with the way she has added detail to the leaf, and stripes on the jumper. She is demonstrating a 'core and radial' schema with the head and hair, the flower and the pig. She does not yet have the open semicircle in her drawing which is a typical indication of readiness for independent efforts at writing. This may be another reason why she wants to copy the rhyme. This is why she is not yet at level 3 in her writing in relation to the Foundation Stage Profile. Her drawings and independent writing of her name suggest to the practitioners 'that she is heading towards that, though she is very comfortably within Phase two'.

Where does the alphabet come in?

We can see that learning the alphabet is of limited use to Lucy at this point in her development and learning. But learning the names of letters in her name will be a useful and emotionally engaging start. The names of letters should always be learnt in the context of written words, rhymes, poems, stories and environmental notices and messages. This is because the letter is not about the sound. A letter name is a general name, which does not change. On the other hand, the 'e' in 'egg' sounds completely different to the sound of the 'e' in 'eel'. Letter names are a constant in a world of changing phonemes/graphemes. They are anchors.

This links with Loui, earlier in the chapter, writing the card for his childminder. Jeni Riley points out how studies with a focus on teaching 'the alphabet by rote, had no enduring value and this fails to guarantee an early successful start to reading. The appreciation of the symbolic representation of letters for spoken sounds occurs slowly over time and with exposure to meaningful experiences of print and text' (Riley, 1999: 58).

Since the days of John Locke's alphabet blocks, and probably before, children have delighted in letter names. When Lucy points at the letter L on a car with 'L' plates, and says, 'That's my name!' we might say something along the lines of, 'Yes,' that's the letter L (pronounced "el"). In your name it sounds "Le", L-u-cy'.

If we do not respond, we are rejecting Lucy's literacy understanding rather than building on it. In the same way, Loui picked out the letters in Julie's name that were the

Skye finds the sound 'S' as in Skye. The children enjoy the garden alphabet, and spontaneously think of words starting with each sound. Ollie said, 'H – Humza'. He thought a moment and then said, 'Happy, hug, hurry up – hurry up and do it! HOG!'

The boy writes his name on the flagstones in chalk. He often returns to his name and stands on it

Experimenting with writing a label for the organic garden

same as his, but may not yet be mapping the sounds onto the letters (graphemes).

Chanting the alphabet is only useful when you are already familiar with how it works. It is useful, with 6- and 7-year-olds, to sing alphabet songs.

Writing does not always have to be on paper

In the photographs you will see boys mark-making in relation to their names on the flag-stones in the garden. This is significant. Boys often do not enjoy mark-making on paper as much as girls do. The boys have asked the adult to write their names in chalk. They then run away and return to stand on their name. They seem to be echoing some of the graphic forms in their own spontaneous mark-making near where the adult has written names.

Although most of the settings, as one practitioner describes it, offer children 'a wide range of activities and resources to promote mark-making and encourage the children to experiment with their own writings and labelling … there is more interest shown by boys this year'.

Boys responded to the three-dimensional, movement-packed opportunities for mark-making and writing. In the photograph opposite you can see a boy quietly engaged in watching the practitioner writing the rhyme 'Humpty Dumpty' on the ground outside. He was very familiar with the rhyme, having actively played with props and taken part in a large-scale drama of the rhyme. Boys often prefer to be outside as they learn.

Going with nature and not against it

It is enjoyable for young children to 'write' using plastic letters, and the keyboards of computers are very attractive to them too. However, as Blakemore and Frith (2005) point out, if children write with pencils and paper, they need to be able to co-ordinate their fingers. The motor cortex, which controls hand/finger co-ordination, is not usually matured and developed in this respect until at least five years of age. This comes later in boys than in girls. Many of the boys we worked with were summer born. These findings have far-reaching implications for 4-year-olds in reception classes.

Sarah-Jayne Blakemore and Uta Frith (2005: 71) suggest that the letter shapes most used today are Roman in origin, and well suited to being stone inscriptions. Some of the letters are mirror-reversible, which makes them confusing.

b.....d
p.....q

The writing area has been carefully set up to attract and engage boys and girls

If we think of them as solid objects in a three-dimensional world, we can twist them around and see they are the same shapes. It is only when they go onto two-dimensional paper that we cannot twist them, and so they have to be written in a certain spatial relationship. 'The mappings between symbols and speech have to be learned, and this learning has a lasting impact on the brain' (Blakemore and Frith, 2005: 71).

People who can read, decode words automatically, even if they have no intention of reading the word. Stroop pre-

The boy is watching the adult writing the rhyme 'Humpty Dumpty' on the ground outside

sented people with lists of words written in different colours, and asked them to name the colour of each word. Some of the words were the names of colours –

Blue
Purple.

It took people longer to read these. 'This is because before you name the colour of the ink you involuntarily read the word, and the meaning comes to mind unbidden. Once you have learned to read, you cannot help but read the meaning of the words (Blakemore and Frith, 2005: 71–2). A child who has reached the stage of being an automatic reader does two things at the same time:

- identifies whole words
- translates the letters into sounds.

A large European collaborative study, using brain-scanning techniques, by neuro-scientists Paulesu, Demonet and Frith, points out that the reader uses one or other of three areas of the brain. But they lean a little more heavily on some more than others, depending on the writing system used. This fits with the findings of Goswami. 'When learning to read English or French, more work is done by the region of the brain responsible for whole word recognition. When learning to read Italian, more work is done by the region that is responsible for letter-sound translation' (Blakemore and Frith, 2005: 79).

Getting the idea of flow in writing

Practitioners in one of the settings had been particularly interested in the way that reading and writing are intertwined.

They often scribed for children when they wanted to retell a story that had been read to them previously. This is the story Rhianna (4 years and 4 months) retold:

The Elves and the Shoemaker

One day there was a shoemaker and his wife. They was very poor.

He cut some shoes and left them on the workbench. He was surprised to see some shoes but he didn't know who did sew them. So a rich lady came and put shoes on. She said they were perfect.

She gave the shoemaker a big bag of money. He cut two pairs of shoes and left them on the bench.

A rich man came into the shops. He said, 'I'll take both pairs.' He gave the shoemaker two big bags of money.

Every time he found perfect shoes on his workbench, he cut shoes out and left them on his workbench.

They hide in a cupboard. Two elves went in the clothes were really old. They made some shoes. The wife saw the old clothes and made tiny new one ready.

Next time 'We like our clothes,' said the elves.

'We like our shoes,' said the wife.

The end

The practitioner wrote: 'Rhianna knew I was scribing her story, and waited after retelling a page of the story for me to catch up on my writing. She can write her name clearly and fluently.'

Both Lucy and Rhianna can write their names independently. But, because the adult writes down what they want to say, they are kept from the frustration of not being able to write whole chunks independently:

- Lucy used a poetry card to copy words she could not write independently.
- The adult provides a rich literacy environment as part of the enabling environment.
- Rhianna found a helpful adult to scribe the retelling of the story.

We found in every setting that the child's name was emotionally important and usually the first word they wrote. We saw in an earlier chapter that Sylvia Ashton-Warner pioneered the importance of words packed with feelings.

David Crystal (2006: 167–9) reports the British Council (2004) world survey of what he calls 'wordmelodies'. They either sound beautiful (blossom, lullaby, kangaroo) or mean something beautiful (mother, eternity).

Emotionally important words are the stuff of creative writing and poetry making. We did not want to neglect this aspect of writing. It is a sad reflection of the way most children are taught to read and write, that they do not become lifelong writers for the sheer pleasure of it. Writing takes huge effort, but it should be worthwhile and satisfying effort. It should foster creative energy and give it space to blossom.

Children often want to write their name on models they make. This often develops so that they want to write about the model

From a three-dimensional world to a two-dimensional world

What happens before children reach the point where they are trying to write their name and other emotionally important words?

Loui, who is 2 years and six months old, gives us some clues (see the drawing on page 78). His childminder writes about his drawing:

> After playing 'Row, row, row your boat', we did some drawing. Loui said 'Julie Boat'. I said, 'Just like the song 'Row, row, row your boat'. Loui said, 'Draw crocodile, draw crocodile,' holding out his pen. I drew the crocodile. Loui covered over his eye and teeth, 'Where boat gone?' said Loui. Then he said, 'Where crocodile gone?' I asked, 'Is it hiding?' Loui says, 'No – gone'.

Let us unpick this. From about 5 or so months old until age 2 or 3 years children are fascinated by peekaboo games. This is about all sorts of things, but one of them is the way they are sorting out that people and objects can be placed over or behind each other. At first, it seems that someone has disappeared, but they are still there behind a cloth.

They seem to be saying, two things, a person and a cloth or curtain, cannot both occupy the same space, so what is happening here? Has the person gone away? But they are still there!

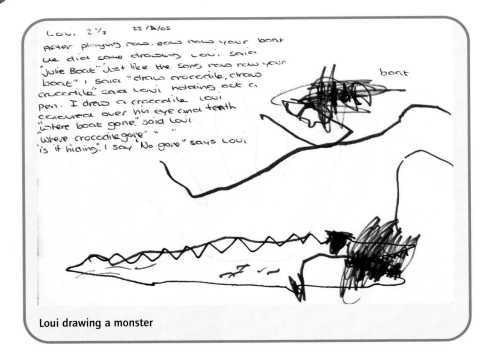

Loui drawing a monster

Piaget (1962) describes this as the development of permanence of the object. As this becomes established, the delight in the game seems to increase, and toddlers love to 'play' with permanence.

Walking, talking and pretending

Walking, talking and pretending come together, in a wonderful cluster with far-reaching consequences for the development and learning of the child.

Loui is at this point. He has understood that you can take a three-dimensional thing (in this case a crocodile) and draw it. Just as Rhianna needed someone else to scribe for her, he needs someone to draw the crocodile. He then does what he can manage, which is to cover the crocodile. He does this by colouring over it. He plays with the idea of hiding or gone (the concept of permanence). It is safer to make the crocodile disappear! Emotion is always there when we work with young children.

This is rehearsal for putting words, which are three-dimensional sounds, into two-dimensional graphemes. He is on the literacy journey towards selecting the right symbols for the situation.

Templates and colouring in outlines: damaging the journey into writing

Piaget (1962) talks about the importance of personal symbols, as the beginnings of writing. Drawings are often not recognizable in what they represent, but they are representational nevertheless.

We need to encourage the child to make personal symbols. These are the bridge to conventional symbols of written texts.

John Matthews (2003) argues that children benefit from adults helping children in their early attempts to do this, but it is unhelpful to give children templates or to require them to colour in outlines. That gives a child the message 'You can't draw! So you had better use this drawing instead of doing your own'.

From personal symbols towards real writing

Lizzie is further into her journey into writing than Loui, but she is 3 years and 7 months old. She has been interested in her family of late, and whether she will still be Lizzie when she grows up.

We can see Loui benefits from an older child drawing independently and with confidence and pleasure. Mixing ages of children is a very positive thing. Older children love to show younger children how they do things, and to explain them, and younger children see what lies ahead without pressure to perform.

Is it significant that Lizzie refers to mummy as 'Middle'? She has been singing

This is Daddy. He has really long legs. He is the biggest. Daddy's hair goes all the way round. He looks like a lion. Mummy is Middle. She has lots of long hair and long legs. Hannah looks like a penguin. I will give her only one eye and hair. Penguins do have hair. These are Philip's legs. They are really long. I will put his head at the bottom. I have eyes, eye-lashes, nose, mouth, hair and ears. I'm the smallest

the finger rhyme 'Peter pointer' with the childminder. It may well be that she is using the analogy of her fingers and their names to look at the heights of people in her family. Goswami (1998) points out that children use analogies as a powerful tool for thinking.

Jeni Riley (2007: 81) emphasizes the importance of an enabling environment indoors and outdoors as a general backcloth to reading and writing, with continuity in the provision of a rich, broad and deep language and literacy environment throughout the *Early Years Foundation Stage* (DfES, 2007a) and through to 7 years.

KEY MESSAGES ABOUT CHILDREN BEGINNING TO WRITE

- Writing draws on language, thoughts, feelings and relationships, but it is more distanced and remote than talking with people.
- Children need to know what writing is about, and what it is for, surrounded by people who enjoy and take writing as a serious pleasure.
- Having something you want to say in writing (composing) is different from the mechanics of writing and forming letters (transcribing).
- Early finger rhymes help the physical aspects of writing to develop. They enhance biological development.
- Larger movements with the shoulders and whole body are also important (see chapters on action songs and enabling learning environments).
- Handwriting is not writing. Handwriting is how the letters are formed. Until children are spontaneously producing the open semicircle in their drawings and mark-making, it is not appropriate to formally teach them lower casement letter formation. But they often enjoy building words with loose alphabets.
- Children should not be pressurized into writing before the motor cortex is sufficiently mature, but they should experience enabling environments, with positive relationships respected as the unique people they are. Practitioners who are working with other people's children need to acquire and update the subject knowledge involved in the mechanics of writing and the creativity, information and pleasure it brings.

Chapter 6

Action Songs – on the Spot

Why sing action songs with young children?

Sometimes the things we do with children, as part of our everyday practice, become such a habit that we no longer give them much of our attention. Students, in their training, learn a selection of songs, often by observing and taking part in group times led by experienced practitioners.

This chapter looks at the importance of action songs which use the upper body or the upper and lower body co-ordinating together – but sitting or staying on the spot (non-locomotion). In the next chapter we look at action songs involving locomotion.

It is useful to stand back from everyday practice, and review it, to take stock and really give it some thought.

- Why has the tradition lasted for over a hundred years?
- Who started it?
- Is it a valuable tradition in this day and age?

Who started the tradition of singing action songs with children?

Friedrich Froebel, who was born in 1782 and died in 1852, pioneered action songs as well as finger rhymes. His influence, though not many people realize this, remains in the action songs we sing daily with children.

Why does the tradition continue today? Is it still a valuable tradition?

Action songs encourage creativity, memory, sensitivity to others, co-ordinated movement, communication, increased vocabulary, language development, music, dance, drama, as well as sequencing, predicting and awareness of detail and anticipation.

However, because this book is about the essentials of literacy, this chapter and chapter 7 emphasize the way that action songs help:

- using the body as a symbol
- listening to rhyming patterns
- appreciating the traditional canon of rhymes in the English language
- co-ordinating body movements while singing
- the links between gross and fine motor skills
- the use of the body as a musical instrument, connecting and co-ordinating different parts of the brain
- phonological awareness
- rhythm
- rhyme
- alliteration
- sequencing
- extending gaze from tracking to a fine, fixed focus on detail.

The upper body: non-locomotion action songs

Feeling grounded and keeping the midline

In the chapter on baby songs, we explored the co-ordinated use of hands, eyes and hearing, which is important for later reading and writing.

Being grounded on the floor, stable, balanced and with the midline is important when singing and moving to action songs using the upper body. It helps children to co-ordinate the upper part of their bodies enough to do the actions. (Kuhlman and Schweinhart, 1999.

The links between gross and fine motor movements

Children need both. That is what we mean by a rich, enabling, multi-sensory learning environment for developing their learning in their unique journeys into literacy. This is given emphasis in the *EYFS* (DfES, 2007a) which has statutory force.

Action songs help children to become symbol users

When children, even very young children who are just beginning to walk, talk and pretend, are introduced to action songs, they begin to understand that one thing can be made to stand for another.

Children with hearing impairments are helped, as they begin to learn signs together with the spoken language which is more challenging for them. The signing helps the spoken language along.

Children with visual impairments also enjoy the movements, and this helps their ability to locate their own body in space, and to develop better mobility. It is very challenging for a child who cannot see to progress from on-the-spot action songs to locomotion action songs, with upper and lower body co-ordinating. (This is explored in the next chapter.) Mobility is a great challenge for children with visual impairments.

Holding a steady beat is important for developing the essentials of literacy and for life as a whole

Action songs help children to co-ordinate the upper and lower body in movement and song so that they learn to locate themselves and their personal tempo in relation to the sounds, tunes, words and movements of others. Holding a steady beat is part of this.

Holding a steady beat is important in developing sensitivity of communication, in hearing the sounds, tones and rhythms of language needed for literacy. It is also in music, dance, drama, sport and life in general. Penny Greenland (2006) describes this in relation to the 'felt sense of self' in the movements of the body.

Keeping a steady beat

Research (Ellis, 1992) shows that young children vary in their responses to a steady beat:

- patting knees with both hands
- clapping
- patting knees with alternate hands
- patting knee with preferred hand
- patting knee with non-preferred hand
- stepping to the toe and stepping back
- walking on the spot.

We all have a natural and personal tempo. 'This personal "timing" is the natural tempo at which the individual relates and reacts to the world' (Kuhlman and Schweinhart, 1999: 14).

It is easier for young children to keep a steady beat when the tempo is at or near their personal tempo

Children aged 3 to 9 years found it easier to keep a steady beat to a faster tune than when the tune was slow. 'The task of synchronising movement with music played slower than an individual's personal tempo is more difficult for that individual than the task of synchronising movement with music played faster than the individual's personal tempo' (Walter, in Kuhlman and Schweinhart, 1999: 3).

Head to feet – the order in which the brain develops co-ordinated movement

Co-ordinating the upper and lower body movements while singing or chanting

In their paper, Kuhlman and Schweinhart (1999) gather together a range of research of suggesting that children with poor control of their legs and feet (tripping and clumsy) often have incomplete cephalocaudal motor development. This means their upper body movements are more developed than their lower body movements, and the two are not well co-ordinated.

Young children, because of their point of biological maturation and development, will find it easier to use their upper body. They will need plenty of opportunities to do this. Action songs sitting or standing on the spot help this along. They are important from the time a child can walk until children are 7 years old. They tend to be sung at a fast tempo, which fits the natural tempo of most young children.

Dressing up clothes help to create the right atmosphere

Because the co-ordination of movements of the upper body develops earlier than the lower body (Kuhlman and Schweinhart, (1999)), children at the end of the Foundation Stage do not always have the same personal tempo in their top and bottom halves.

They may well be beginning to be able to clap to a fast or slow beat of an action song with success, holding the beat steady. This is because the upper body is becoming more co-ordinated. But they might need a faster song if they are to move about, because their feet and legs cannot slow down while holding a steady beat and step.

The body is the first musical instrument

Children who learn to play musical instruments later on are at an advantage in their education, but action songs are the earlier version of musical instruments. The body is the first musical instrument.

As children sing, they need to give the movements of the song at the same time. Their body accompanies their singing.

So that children can manage in the early stages of this action song, practitioners often get the children to sit in a circle around the princess (in the action song 'A princess lived in a high tower') and to do the actions with their upper bodies. Later on, as the children become able to do the actions while singing the words, they can move round in a circle as they sing and do the actions. But this requires them not only to control and manage their own body, singing and looking, but also to be aware of where they are moving in relation to others in a circle dance. It helps children if they can have plenty of experience with non-locomotion action songs. However, the biological maturation of the body also comes into this. Children aged from 4 to 7 years are at the point where this is an important part of their developing learning.

When children sing an action song, it means that, in their head, they have to pitch notes just ahead of each sound they sing or chant. Sally Goddard-Blythe (2004: 87) says this means children have to:

A small group do on action song on the mat

- visualize the sound
- anticipate the use of the internal ear
- motor plan where their actions will be
- respond to other people singing and action moving alongside them in the group
- combine all of this so that sensory motor skills integrate with feedback continuously back to the ear and the eye.

All this will be invaluable in giving children key ways of making the journey into sensitive communicating with others, talking and listening with others with engagement and focus, and reading and writing later on.

Phonological awareness

Children need to become phonologically aware if they are to move without difficulty into later reading. Phonological awareness is a global term (Mallett, 2005). It means becoming aware of similarities and differences in sounds and their patterns, tones, tempo and beat, loudness, softness, the source of the sound and the sounds.

Becoming phonologically aware helps children along their journey into literacy. It paves the way for them to become **phonemically aware**. Being phonemically

The children are integrating the sounds and the actions so that **ears** and **eyes** are working together through **movement**. This will help them later in reading and writing, when the eye and the ear need to work in a co-ordinated way

aware is all about hearing and being able to recognize the different phonemes (sounds) in a word (Mallett, 2005: 243).

Phonemes are the smallest units of sound in a word

In the next chapters we shall look at how developing both broad phonological and more detailed phonemic awareness help children to get the most out of learning nursery rhymes, poetry cards and story or information books. All this will be happening in a richly enabling learning environment both indoors and outdoors, where relationships are positive and children are respected as unique individuals (DfES, 2007a).

Rhythm

A simple action song helps to see how a child is developing, understanding and confident in the art of pattern-making. Songs and their accompanying actions provide opportunities for children to learn to express themselves with confidence, socially in a group or alone at home with their families.

Singing action songs with children is enormous fun, but it is much more than that. It helps the brain to process some of the things that will be of key importance in developing the ability to talk, listen, develop good language and vocabulary, and to read and write. Developing a sense of rhythm is part of this.

Sally Goddard-Blythe (2004: 68) points out that both rhythm and sound are created as a result of movement. She says that:

- rhythm is a sequence of movements in time
- sound is made from vibrations.

Moving while you sing is therefore very important for young children, and especially for children with special needs and disabilities. Adam Ockelford, a musician, educator and academic working with children with visual impairments and complex needs, has found that singing with actions is helpful. Let us take an action song like:

Roly poly, roly poly, up, up, up,
Roly poly, roly poly, down, down, down,
Roly poly, roly poly give a little clap,
Roly poly, roly poly, sit like that.

The child experiences the words 'up', 'down' and 'clap' through the movements. This is done in a sequence of sounds arranged in a pattern, which is called a **rhythm**.

The regular metred pattern is called the beat. Ros Bayley has developed the sense of **beat** in a rhythm through her songs for a puppet called 'Beat Baby'. In this case, an object is used to create a rhythmic accompaniment to a rhyme. Action songs create movements to accompany the words of the rhyme or song.

The arms go up in the beat of the words, going up a little higher each time the word 'up' is said. Both are important, but the feedback, through movements while singing, give powerfully integrated messages to the brain.

Rhyme

Children have a strong sense of rhyme, if encouraged to keep and develop this. With all brain functions it is a case of 'use it or lose it'. Some cultures place more emphasis on rhyme than others in the way music and dance, poetry and song are part of life for everyone.

Action songs are an introduction to rhyme. They are not about how the rhyme is written down. It is important to realize this, because there are many words in the English language which sound similar and rhyme, but which look quite different when written down.

Rhyme supports phonemic awareness

English is one of the most irregular, difficult languages in the world. Usha Goswami (2005; 2006) has researched this in some detail. She suggests that it is at its most irregular with the smallest units of sound (phonemes) but it is much more regular with the larger units of rhyming chunks of sound. This links with the cross-cultural research of Uta Frith and colleagues, which we explored in the chapter on writing.

Morag Stuart (2007), in a lecture suggested that we need to know as much as we can about the contribution phonic knowledge makes to a child's development in the journey into literacy, suggesting that many words children find in books they are given to read are regular. However, Dominic Wyse and Morag Styles (2007: 21) argue that an emphasis on synthetic phonics is wrong, and that a more balanced approach to reading needs to prevail. Sue Ellis (2007: 41) supports this, pointing out most teachers are not 'exercised about the analytic/synthetic debate; good teachers respond to the patterns and possibilities children notice, and in practice the distinction is rarely as clear cut as theorists would believe'.

Rhyme engages a child's attention

There could be some agreement here between the different points of view. It is not just a question of the frequency with which children come across words and rhyming chunks. It is also the meaning and pleasure given by rhyme. The brain has a propensity for patterns. Rhymes engage children (and adults) and we know that singing helps this process along.

Children need rhyming chunks to support the development of letter–sound correspondences and the processes of blending and segmenting. They make it easier for children to enjoy and engage with texts later on. They provide powerful ways for children to focus, listen, look, move and integrate these in ways that support reading and writing.

This is why it is important to give children rich language environments indoors and outdoors, with real and multi-sensory experiences.

The challenge for those of us working with young children is how to make it as easy as possible for children to communicate using the English language, and to help them in their journey into reading and writing so that they are not just dutiful readers and writers, but avid and enthusiastic bookworms and writers.

Hearing the patterns of the rhymes

The beauty of action songs is that they are not presented to children in a written down form. We 'act' them out with the children. They contain rhymes, with words that have similar sound patterns and rhythms. 'Roly' sounds very similar to 'poly' in the action song. Children learn to hear the sameness in these words. They also begin to distinguish between the 'R' of Roly and the 'P' of Poly. This will be very important for later learning to read print.

The children sing while they do the actions. It helps them to sit on the floor to do this, so that they can use the upper body without having to co-ordinate it with the lower body

When singing action songs, because they are not written down when presented to the children, the focus is on the patterns of sound which make the rhymes. There is no text to look at, so it not an issue that there are many words which rhyme in sound, but look different when written down. This means that some of the words in the songs sound the same, but are not spelt the same. Because the emphasis is on how the words sound in an action song, this does not matter.

In the photograph you can see the children singing the action song, 'Wind the bobbin'. The boys and the girls are engaged and focused as they sing and do the actions. The adults in the pre-school playgroup have spaced themselves out so that children can watch and imitate an adult wherever they are sitting.

Wind the bobbin

Wind the bobbin up
Wind the bobbin up
Pull, pull, clap, clap, clap.

Point to the ceiling
Point to the floor
Point to the ceiling
Point to the floor.

Clap your hands together
One, two, three
Put your hands upon your knee.

Children need to be encouraged to concentrate at their own pace

The children are pointing to the ceiling as they sing the action song. The adult is looking at the end of her finger as she sings, and is exaggerating this movement so as to encourage it. Two girls are doing this. Other children are doing the action without tracking it with their eyes. One girl is slower to raise her arm, but is very focused and engaged. Several children are singing but not doing the actions.

We need to remember, as Sally Goddard-Blythe demonstrates, that it is very challenging for the children to co-ordinate the actions and the singing. They need plenty of repetition on different days in order to do this. Some children in the group are very young, just having turned 3 years old. They should not be rushed or nagged.

This is why it is a good idea to have **small groups** of children, so that adults can go at the right pace for the children singing the song. This gives children who are just beginning to take part in action-song singing the time to get the movements co-ordinated with the singing. It is easier to get it right with a small group. When practitioners work with large groups, inevitably some children get lost, and there is a tendency to treat children as a herd to be driven along!

Extending the gaze

At first, babies gaze at faces, and enjoy being talked to and sung to at this close distance.

The extended gaze goes from:

- face to face
- face to hands
- face to end of arms
- face to end of toes.

Seeing things at a more distant focus is important in reading print later on. Action songs are helpful in this. Babies watch their arms go up or down, and then they focus on the hand.

Action songs using the body, but on the spot (non-locomotion)

There are many action songs of this type. In the first stage they are sung sitting on the floor (so that the child is grounded and not having to

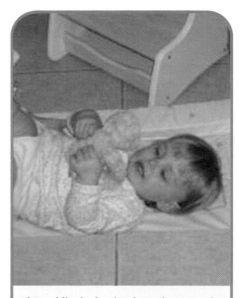

The toddler looks closely at the toy and holds it up. Later, the gaze near and far will be further developed through action songs

balance on a chair). The position is upright. The arms and hands and fingers of the upper body are the main focus. It is challenging for children to sing and do the actions at the same time. Adults often offer songs where the movements are too difficult to do at the same time as singing. If you consistently find yourself singing a solo, think again! Is this matching the child's development?

Stage 1 action songs – upper body, simple rhymes and movements

We have looked at '**Wind the bobbin up**' (**object type**) earlier in the chapter. This is a stage 1 action song. Here are some more. They include songs from nature, about objects and people in the Froebelian tradition.

As always an action song such as 'Five little ducks' means more if real ducks have been experienced

Incy wincy spider (animal type)

Incy wincy spider
Climbed up the spout. (Use the fingers of both hands to represent the spider climbing the spout)

Down came the rain
And washed the spider out. (Raise the hands and lower them slowly, wriggling fingers to be the rain)

Out came the sunshine
Dried up all the rain. (Raise the hands above the head together and spread them out and then down again)

And Incy wincy spider
Climbed the spout again. (The same as the first lines)

As children become more experienced with upper body, non-locomotion action songs, the actions can become more complex.

Stage 2 action songs – more upper body movement sequences and several verses

These are still:

- on the spot
- non-locomotion
- involving the upright position.

However, the movements involve:

- more complex sequences of movement to remember
- several verses to sing.

In the baby song 'Round and round the garden', (see photograph on page 89), the parent performs the actions for the child. Here the child does their own actions. There is progression.

Little cottage in the wood

(Make roof with hands)

Little girl at the window stood
(Look through holes when a circle is made out of the thumb and forefinger)

Saw a rabbit running by
(Pound on the floor with feet)

Knocking at the door
(Knock one fist on the palm of the other hand)

'Help me, help me' the rabbit cried
(Hands up and down in the air)

'Or the hunter will shoot me dead.'
(Pretend to aim and shoot)

Little rabbit come inside
(Beckon with forefinger)

You'll be safe with me
(Hold the rabbit like a baby in folded arms)

The story element helps children to remember the narrative (important for later reading). The actions, such as the feedback to the brain of the fist on the palm of the hand are important for later writing.

Stage 3 – whole-body non-locomotion action songs

The selection of action songs using the whole body is carefully made to illustrate the range. Different movements, involving the co-ordination of the upper and lower body are used.

Keeping the midline

We all clap hands together

We all clap hands together
We all clap hands together
Because it's fun to do

We all stand up together
We all sit down together
We all stamp feet together
We all turn round together

Bending from the middle – the vestibular system

These action songs link to the vestibular system in the body. They involve the tilting and tipping which Penny Greenland (2000) emphasizes is so important.

The children sit on the floor, and bend forwards and backwards as if rowing. Older children sometimes like to sit one behind the other to do this, giving the impression of all being in a rowing boat and rowing together. However, co-ordinating your movements with someone else, even if they are doing the same thing, is quite a challenge. It might be a challenge too far for very young children! Encouraging children to control their own movements is the thing to concentrate on at this stage.

Row, row, row your boat

Gently down the stream
Merrily, merrily , merrily , merrily
Life is but a dream.

Row, row, row your boat
Gently out to sea
Merrily, merrily, merrily, merrily
We'll be home for tea.

Row, row, row your boat
Gently on the tide
Merrily, merrily, merrily, merrily
To the other side.

Row, row, row your boat
Gently back to shore
Merrily, merrily, merrily, merrily
Home for tea at four.

Bending from the midline to the side

The child holds his or her arm in a curve down one side, and holds out the arm on the other side. This is quite a challenge for young children, because they have to do something different with each arm. They also have to tilt to 'pour' so that the out-held arm points to the floor.

I'm a little teapot

Short and stout
Here's my handle
Here's my spout.
When I see the tea cups
Hear me shout!
Pick me up and pour me out.

Sequences from top to toe

In this song, the same movement action works its way down from the head to the toes. The child is still on the spot but the movement is in a sequence. It is simple in that the same movement is performed each time. The two hands are placed flat on the head, shoulders, and so on. The child has to turn on the spot, which is quite a challenge at first.

Heads, shoulders, knees and toes

Knees and toes, knees and toes
Heads and shoulders, knees and toes
We all turn round together.

This time, the movement is different in each verse, but still involves both sides of the body (hands together, feet doing the same movement, hands doing the same movement, and so on).

If you're happy and you know it

Clap your hands
If you're happy and you know it
Clap your hands
If you're happy and you know it
And you really want to show it
If you're happy and you know it
Clap your hands
If you're happy and you know it
Stamp your feet ... and so on.

If you're happy and you know it
Tap your knees ...

Co-ordinating movements, singing the words and different pitch: loud, soft and normal speaking voice

The actions are relatively simple, but the children need to co-ordinate these with shouting loudly, or whispering softly, and with a normal pitch. Young children find whispering difficult, and the song helps them to make the sound contrasts.

The movements involve shaking the head, wrists and feet, in a particular order. There is the glimmer of a story developing here. Children anticipate the movements as the narrative unfolds through the character of the scarecrow.

I'm a dingle dangle scarecrow

When all the cows were sleeping and the sun had gone to bed,
Up jumped the scarecrow, and this is what he said:
'I'm a dingle-dangle scarecrow with a flippy, floppy hat.
I can shake my hands like this, and shake my feet like that.'

When all the hens were roosting, and the moon behind a cloud,
Up jumped the scarecrow, and shouted very loud:
'I'm a dingle-dangle ...', and so on.

When the dogs were in the kennel, and the doves were in the loft
Up jumped the scarecrow, and whispered very soft:
'I'm a dingle, dangle scarecrow ...', and so on.

IN SUMMARY

Action songs are powerful ways of supporting the development of the essentials of literacy.

- In stages 1 and 2, they challenge children in the co-ordination of the arms and upper body. Movements and verses and narratives become increasingly complex.
- In stage 3, the upper and lower body is used, but on the spot.
- Action songs support the integration of sound, sight and movement.
- They give a gentle introduction to narrative and the development of characters.
- They give a gentle introduction towards singing games.
- They help children with phonological awareness, through alliteration, rhyme and rhythm.

Chapter 7

Action Songs – Moving Around

In this chapter, we shall explore action songs which involve locomotion (travel away from the spot). These involve the integration of movements of the whole body with sight and sound. From the time they sit, babies begin to delight in adults imitating their movements. Over time, toddlers spend time imitating the movements of others in a more conscious way.

We saw how the two (being imitated and imitating) came together in 'Oogly Boogly', the theatre group who aim their work at children on the cusp of speaking. This process continues to develop through the first seven years, and action songs involving locomotion support this in deep ways.

Why locomotion action songs come later

At first, children flail about when performing action songs involving moving around (locomotion). This is because they find it quite difficult to co-ordinate their feet and legs with their arms, hands and heads. It is even more difficult to do all of that and move about in a circle!

The chaotic scene of toddlers being required to perform 'Ring a ring o' roses' and falling over with wild abandon is a frequent occurence. It is simply too difficult for a new walker to manage. It is not going to do any damage, and it can be great fun, but it does mean that the children are not yet ready to co-ordinate a steady beat, both upper and lower halves together.

Honing emerging skills

It is good for older children to be with younger children, so that younger children see the possibilities and what lies ahead. They are eager to be with older children, providing they are not pressurized to perform in advance of their competencies. Older children benefit from thinking of others less able to do what they can do, and helping them. But it is also important that children who are ready to hold a steady beat in locomotion action songs have the opportunity to do this. They need to hone their skills without becoming frustrated and giving up because of always being with younger children. Again, children need both. This is why small-group times are of central importance in getting things right for each unique child.

Co-ordinating movements with other people

Making and dancing in a circle is not an easy thing for very young children to do. It is best to do this in a small group. If children cannot manage this (and 2- and 3-year-olds are challenged to do so) and if trying to make them do this becomes a nagging session, such that the group never gets to sing the song, then abandon it. There are other ways to sing an action song, as we saw in the previous chapter, and you can return to this when the children have more experience and biological maturation. Children need to be experienced, having sung action songs based on their upper body, or on the spot with the whole body (as we explored in the previous chapter), and able to develop sensitivity to moving in relation to each other.

An emergent partner dance

It is more important for children to manage, control and co-ordinate their upper and lower body movements, without having to move with other people in mind. Once they can manage the movements while singing or chanting, they often enjoy joining with others in a dance-like way. Formation dances are early forms of dance, and we can see the glimmerings of this in the photograph of the spontaneous play of the children.

The girls often take the lead in this, but the boys are usually watching them and thoroughly enjoying their performance. Children often spend time observing others before they decide to join in. Practitioners often report that boys often seem to wait and observe in this way more than girls when it comes to singing, dancing, drawing, mark-making and looking at books. But in other areas of development and learning they make the first move, such as in working out mechanical problems and challenges, or in three-dimensional constructions such as wooden blockplay.

Action songs involving locomotion

Travelling action songs

I went to school one morning, and I walked like this

Walked like this, walked like this.
I went to school one morning and I walked like this
All on my way to school.

I saw a little robin and he hopped like this …, and so on.
I saw a shiny river and I splashed like this …, and so on.
I saw a little pony and he galloped like this …, and so on.
I saw a tall policeman and he stood like this …, and so on.

I heard the school bell ringing and I ran like this …, and so on.

Jumping action songs

Three little monkeys jumping on the bed

One fell off and bumped his head.
His Mummy called the doctor
And the doctor said:
'No more monkeys jumping on the bed!'

Two little monkeys were jumping on the bed.
One fell off and bumped his head.
His Mummy called the doctor
And the doctor said:
'No more monkeys jumping on the bed!'

One little monkey jumping on the bed.
He fell off and bumped his head.
His Mummy called the doctor
And the doctor said:
'No more monkeys jumping on the bed!'

Here the actions are the same in each verse, but not all the children take part. Only the monkeys do the jumping. It is best if all the children have a turn at jumping, and so this action song is best with about six children.

Rolling action songs

It is easier to rotate the body by rolling on the floor than it is to turn around when standing up.

There were ten in a bed

And the little one said,
'Roll over! Roll over!'
So they all rolled over
And one fell out.
He gave a little scream 'OW!'
He gave a little shout 'HEY!
That was very mean!'

There were nine in a bed … , and so on.

This song introduces 'voice sounds' and the hint of a story.

Crossing the midline by pointing

Did you ever see a lassie

A lassie, a lassie,
Did you ever see a lassie
Go this way and that?

Go this way and that way,
Go this way and that way,
Did you ever see a lassie
Go this way and that?

Children can sit on the floor, in a circle, and with their hand above their eyebrow, as if saluting, turn their head in either direction, or they can point one way and then the other.

Later, they can do this as they move round in a circle, with one child placed in the centre, as the lassie or the laddie.

Alternate sides

Here we go Looby Loo

Here we go Looby Light,
Here we go Looby Loo,
All on a Saturday night.

You put your left arm in,
You put your left arm out,
You shake it a little, a little,
And turn yourself about

The next verses are:

You put your right arm in ..., and so on.
You put your left leg in ..., and so on

You put your whole self in ..., and so on

Early circle action songs

There are some action songs ('Looby Loo', 'Did you ever see a lassie') which make a good transition from children needing to be in one place and able to focus on their own body doing the actions while singing.

The children can sing this on the spot, or they can move round in a circle, singing for the chorus, and then stop to do the action. This helps them to manage the movements without having to worry about getting round in a circle, and being sensitive to what others are doing and where they are placed in the circle.

Here we go round the mulberry bush

> The mulberry bush, the mulberry bush,
> Here we go round the mulberry bush
> On a cold and frosty morning.

Children walk round in a circle, singing the chorus above. Then they stand still, and focus on doing the actions with their upper body only, as they sing:

> This is the way we wash our hands,
> Wash our hand, wash our hands,
> This is the way we wash our hands,
> On a cold and frosty morning.

They repeat the circle movements singing the chorus again, and then stop to sing the next more focused movements as they sing.

> This is the way we wash our face …
>
> This is the way we comb our hair …
>
> This is the way we tie our shoes …

In this way the circle game is manageable for young children.

A much loved, but later locomotion song is the 'Hokey Cokey'. It involves standing still to do the more focused actions, with running forward and backwards, or walking in a circle holding hands in between. It is more difficult to go forwards and backwards like this than the simpler walking round in a circle holding hands in the 'Mulberry Bush' earlier form of locomotion action song.

Hokey, Cokey   Children hold hands in a circle and walk round singing:

> Oh, do the hokey, cokey.
> Oh, do the hokey, cokey.
> Oh, do the hokey, cokey,
> Knees bend, arms stretch,
> Ra, ra, ra.

Then they stand on the spot and do the actions:

> You put your left arm in,
> You put your left arm out,
> In, out, in out and shake it all about.
> You do the Hokey Cokey and you turn around,
> And that's what it's all about.

Then chorus again, with joined hands, run into the middle and retreat backwards, still holding hands. Release hands and do the actions with knees bend, and so on.

The next verses are:

You put your right arm in ...
You put your left leg in ...
You put your right leg in ...
You put your whole self in ...

Action songs that become ring games

Ring games involve children in rules which have an element of choice (Kalliala, 2005). An early and simple form is:

Sandy Girl

There's a little sandy girl
Sitting on a stone
Crying, crying, because she's all alone.
Stand up, sandy girl
Dry your tears away
Chose one to be your friend
And come out to play.

A boy or girl (or both can be sandy people) sit in the centre of the circle with their hands over their eyes. The children walk round in a circle singing. Sandy people choose a child each to hold with both hands. They then turn round together on the spot, holding hands. The chosen children then go into the centre to become the sandy people.

A later, more complex form of ring game is:

In and out the dusty bluebells

In and out the dusty bluebell
In and out the dusty bluebells
In and out the dusty bluebells
You shall be my partner.

Tippy, tappy, tippy, tappy on my shoulder,
Tippy, tappy. Tippy, tappy on my shoulder,
Tippy, tappy, tippy, tappy on my shoulder,
You shall be my partner.

The children form a circle, and join hands making arches.

One child runs in and out of the arches, and stops behind one of the children. The child touched comes out of the circle and, holding the shoulder of the one who chose them, follows in and out of the arches. All the children make a line in the end. This is a ring game. It involves children in choices in relation to the rules of the game. It also has elements of a formation dance, like those found in folk dances.

Ring games involving running

I sent a letter to my friend

And on the way I dropped it
One of you has picked it up
And put it in your pocket.
It wasn't you, it wasn't you
… It was you!

The children sing as they walk round in a circle, and then they sit on the floor at the end of the verse. One has a piece of paper to represent the letter. This child walks round the outside of the circle, saying 'It wasn't you … and then drops it behind one of the children. This child jumps up and runs after the child who dropped the letter, trying to race them back to the empty space and sit in it. The child left without a space to sit in picks up the letter and the song begins again.

This song, because it is more complex (as is 'Dusty Bluebells'), is suitable for children when they are about 6 or 7 years old.

Action songs that create a drama

An action song that tells a story, is 'A *Princess lived in a High Tower*'.

The photographs tell the story. Every culture seems to have different versions around this literary theme. In fact, all the finger rhymes and action songs in the book are cross-cultural in their themes. There are similar rhymes and songs everywhere in the world. The different languages of the world have their own rhythms, rhymes and sounds. Through these, children learn their culture, their language and are helped in their journey towards literacy. In this book we are thinking about how the particular action songs selected help and support children to learn the tones and feel of the English language. However, it is also invaluable to teach children action songs in different languages, so that their experience goes beyond English alone.

Stories like 'Rapunzel', and 'Sleeping Beauty' are more complex forms of this action song. These themes of literature are cross-cultural. The action song introduces the theme in a very engaging, easy-to-understand way. It is as if it gives the headlines for the more sophisticated version.

Verse 1
The princess stands in the centre of the ring of children:

There was a princess long ago, long ago,
Long ago.
There was a princess long ago, long ago.

There was a princess long, long ago

She lived in a big high tower

A great big forest grew around

Verse 2

The children raise their hands to make a tower:

> And she lived in a big high tower,
> A big high tower, a big high tower,
> And she lived in a big high tower,
> Long ago.

Verse 3

One child, as the fairy, waves her arm over the princess:

> One day a fairy waved her wand, waved her wand,
> Waved her wand,
> One day a fairy waved her wand, waved her wand.

Verse 4

The princess lies down and closes her eyes:

> The princess slept for a hundred years, a hundred years,
> A hundred years,
> The princess slept for a hundred years,
> A hundred years.

Verse 5

The children wave their arms like trees:

> A great big forest grew around, grew around,
> Grew around,
> A great big forest grew around, grew around.

Verse 6

One child, as the prince, gallops round the outside of the ring:

> A gallant prince came riding by, riding by,
> Riding by,
> A gallant prince came riding by,
> Riding by.

Verse 7

He pretends to cut down the trees:

He cut the trees down with his sword, with
his sword,
With his sword.
He cut the trees down with his sword,
With his sword.

Verse 8
He wakes up the princess:

He took her hand to wake her up, wake
her up,
Wake her up,
He took her hand to wake her up,
Wake her up.

Verse 9
Children skip round clapping their
hands:

So everyone is happy now, happy now, happy
now
So everyone is happy no, happy now.

Using play props to revisit the song

In the next chapter, we look at the importance of nursery rhymes and the use of dressing-up clothes and props in helping children on their journey into traditional English literature and literacy. These help children to hear the sounds of the English language. Throughout the book it is important to note that these are located within the richness of an enabling learning environment, which will include songs and music and dance from diverse cultures.

In the photographs of the princess in her tower, you can see how the children have raided the dressing-up box and found appropriate clothes for the characters. It is important that children have opportunities to revisit action songs, nursery rhymes and other songs in their own time and in their own way. Not all children come alive when they are in an

He cut the trees down with his sword

He took her hand to wake her up

Everyone is happy now

adult-led group. They may appreciate trying out the songs in a more private context, quietly with a few friends, or alone. A carefully selected dressing-up area is therefore important (see Chapter 2).

Is it worth continuing the tradition of singing action songs with children?

This is a very easy question to answer. In a word – yes.

IN SUMMARY

Action songs are a sound tradition, worth keeping because they:

- support important developmental processes in the brain, which will be useful and crucial in the journey through communication, language and literacy
- give children powerful ways of engaging with, understanding and participating in cultural events such as community singing and dancing
- contain cross-cultural literary themes which are found throughout the world
- help children to work out what it is to be a symbol user and sing other people's songs and actions, (being a performer) and develop ideas about being a symbol maker, so that they create their own action songs
- act as a bridge from finger rhymes and fine motor control, to story and drama on a larger scale
- give children manageable experiences of rhythm and steady beat in movement and song
- encourage children to remember, imitate and be imitated
- support the integration of on-the-spot and locomotive movement, sight and sound in the English language
- help children to be co-ordinated in their upper and lower bodies, so that, quite literally, they are whole people
- encourage children to create their own action songs
- give children essentials for later literacy.

Chapter 8

Nursery Rhymes

In this chapter we look at stage 1 of the way we can support children through nursery rhymes as they develop the essentials of literacy.
  We focus on:

- the way children have a natural sense of drama. They enjoy the rhymes and the miniature stories they tell. They delight in the characters and situations
- the way they support phonological and phonemic awareness
- how children benefit from sensitive introduction to a core of carefully selected nursery rhymes which can be used to foreground the natural engagement of children (and adults!) with rhythm, rhyme, alliteration and initial sounds
- the need, alongside the small core of nursery rhymes put to specific use, for a wider range of much loved rhymes which, in a less focused way, cover a rich range of literature
- the initial sounds 'b' and 'sh', 'm', 'h', 'd', 'p' and 's', introduced and highlighted through 'Mary', Mary quite contrary,' 'Humpty Dumpty' and 'See Saw, Margery Daw'
- the dangers of over-teaching. Children understand before they can perform.

It is important to make sure that children understand the vocabulary and that the rhymes have meaning for them. In Chapter 2 there are examples of how this can be done in an enabling environment with positive relationships.

Nursery rhymes are part of the canon of literature in the English language

Nursery rhymes give children a **canon of literature** which connects them with the traditions of their culture. Every culture has its own equivalent of nursery rhymes. It is important that children are introduced to a wide range of nursery rhymes, tapping into their diversity and richness across the world. 'It is likely that sensitivity to the rhythms and sound patterns of language is a universal feature of all cultures and their languages, as songs, poems, dances and music from around the world all indicate' (Whitehead, 1999: 23).

The sounds of language

Children who grow up speaking and hearing different languages, and who become bilingual and multilingual, are at a great advantage. They are able to pick up on the **phonology** (sound patterns) of different languages with more sensitivity than children who are monolingual. But it is natural for all children, and indeed adults, to be drawn to rhythm, rhyme and alliteration.

In earlier chapters we have seen that the brain is hardwired for the sounds of languages. But, unless children are introduced to rhymes from birth, they are likely to lose, rather than further develop, the range of possibilities for hearing sounds of:

- alliteration (which uses the same or similar sounds at the beginning of words)
- rhyme (which takes the ear to the sounds at the ends of words)
- rhythm (which is about syllabification – the part of a word pronounced as one beat)
- steady beat (this aspect of rhythm is explored in the chapters on action songs)
- phonological awareness (hearing differences and similarities in sounds, such as alliteration, rhyme and rhythms builds up phonological awareness)
- phonemic awareness (being able to hear and recognize phonemes, which are the smallest unit of meaningful sound in a word, also builds up phonological awareness).

The Grand Old Duke of York

Margaret Mallett (2005: 243) suggests that sensitivity to the phonemic structure of spoken words is linked with success in reading. Others agree (Bryant and Bradley, 1985; Clay, 1998; Goswami and Bryant, 1991; Snowling and Hulme, 2007; Stuart, 2006).

Building memorable and meaningful vocabulary – nursery rhymes help

Marian Whitehead (1999: 21) points out that alliteration, rhyme and rhythm help us to remember. In ordinary conversations it is difficult to remember exactly the words we say to each other. Rhymes make it easier to remember. They therefore help children to remember new words and they build vocabulary. Children with narrow language and poor vocabularies have more difficulty in reading and writing.

Introducing a few carefully elected nursery rhymes through which to develop phonemic awareness

In olden days, few children would have encountered books in their homes, but, children were introduced to nursery rhymes which were sung to them. In this way, they developed sensitivity to the sounds which become so important when later they begin to engage with decoding and encoding as they learned to read and write.

Nowadays many children have the advantage of books from a few months of age. The government has a very successful 'Books for Babies' scheme, so that babies receive books before they walk, and as toddlers.

> Experience shows that children benefit hugely by exposure to books from an early age.
> Right from the start, lots of opportunities should be provided for children to engage with books that fire their imagination and interest. They should be encouraged to choose and peruse books freely as well as sharing them when read by an adult.
> Enjoying and sharing books leads to children seeing them as a source of pleasure and interest and motivates them to value reading. (DfES, Letters and Sounds 2007b: 2)

This is where nursery rhymes are so helpful. Singing these, and using props so that children can connect with them in a three-dimensional way, helps children to develop focus so that they engage with the sounds and actions, with the phonological awareness that is needed to later read and write.

Children are helped when:

Mary, Mary Quite Contrary's garden. Some play props

- baby songs are introduced in three stages
- action songs are introduced in three stages
- nursery rhymes are introduced in two stages.

Nursery rhymes – stage 1: phonemic awareness

This means helping children to hear and distinguish the smallest units of sounds in words. Listening to the words and sounds so that children distinguish between and recognize the alliterations, rhythms and rhymes helps this process along. The nursery rhyme is first introduced, sung and acted out, and props are used. The text is not emphasized at this stage. This does not mean that children should be deprived of the print form of the nursery rhyme, but it does mean that the sounds are the focus, and not the print. This is the message in this chapter. It is important to choose a small core of nursery rhymes which highlight phonemic awareness.

Bye Baby Bunting

Quiet pride in showing the model she has made of Humpty's wall

Others can be enjoyed in a more general way, rather than in the specific ways focused on in this chapter.

Nursery rhymes – stage 2

Poetry cards (next chapter) are introduced in which the rhymes are regular in spelling throughout the rhyme. Children are presented with large cards, with pictures illustrating the rhyme and the text. Attention is drawn to aspects of the text in very incidental and informal ways. This will be explored in the next chapter. Nursery rhymes support phonemic awareness, and help children to map sounds onto graphemes (letters and clusters of letters representing the smallest units of sound – phonemes).

Using nursery rhymes – strengthening what comes naturally to children

Do not pressurize children to articulate sounds that are still biologically developing

It is important to bear in mind that some sounds are more difficult than others for children to make. This is a developmental matter. The following sounds, developed with the guidance of linguists, educators and speech and language experts, are taken from the trainers' booklet, *Communicating Matters* (DfES, 2005a).

As teachers of children with hearing impairments and speech and language specialists know, some of the easiest sounds to hear and say in English are **p, b, m, n** (pronounced as in **pot, baby, Mum** and **no**).

The sounds **h, w, t, d, g, k, y** (pronounced as in **hallo, why?, tomorrow, Dad, Gran, kite, you**) are made by children who are speaking English so that a listener who does not know them well can understand what the child is saying.

By the end of the *Early Years Foundation Stage*, most children are able to blend sounds in English. This means that as they speak they use the sounds **sh, ch, bl, fl, sl, sn, st, cr, gr, sm, str** (as pronounced in **shell, chat, blue, floor, slippery, snake, station, crane, growl, smile strange**). They can usually say the sound 'f'.

But many children entering year 1 in Key Stage 1 do not yet easily say the sounds **l, z, v, s, r, th** (as pronounced in **lap, zoo, vet, sugar, rabbit, thumb**).

Children can hear sounds differences before they can say them

We worked with a speech and language therapist, who emphasized the importance of giving children nursery rhymes with a clear contrast in the phonemes (smallest units of sound in the word). We found that nursery rhymes, with their phonograms (initial sound followed by rhyming chunk), such as 'See Saw, Margery Daw' do this quite naturally. We also found that some nursery rhymes can be quite confusing. Perhaps this is behind the angry and passionate debates about rhyme in recent years. Not all rhymes are helpful. But carefully selected, they give huge and valuable support to children in developing the phonic aspects of reading and writing.

Issues of inclusion and diversity

The outline on the biological development of the sounds children articulate are very general statements. The *Early Years Foundation Stage* principles remind us that children are individuals.

Some children have special needs, learning difficulties and disabilities. Others speak English as an additional language and, if they are new arrivals, the sounds of the English language may be new to them. Some children will have engaged in sensitive communication with adults from birth, with rich language development, able to interact and focus attention in 'shared sustained conversations' (Siraj-Blatchford, et al., 2002). Others have been given puréed food for most of their lives, such that they find chewing difficult and difficulty in forming many of the sounds of English. They may also spend long periods of time in front-facing pushchairs, unable to see faces of adults pushing them, and not spoken to directly for much of the day. Adults might use mobile phones, so that talking is not interactive with the child.

Humpty Dumpty falls over again, and the rhyme is chanted over and over again

Is there an ideal order for helping children to distinguish and hear the sounds of the English language in a way that will help them towards reading and writing?

It makes sense to introduce the sounds important for reading and writing English in ways which help children to discriminate them most easily. Bearing this in mind, we found ourselves on a journey which proved to be fascinating. We wanted to try and link the biologically driven understandings children have of the sounds of the English language with the recommended order of sounds in *Playing with Sounds* (DfES, 2004). This has now been superseded by *Letters and Sounds* (DfES, 2007b) which suggests a completely different order. We were interested to find that some of the easier sounds to produce were suggested for introduction later, and some of the more difficult sounds were suggested for earlier inclusion.

However, the document, which is for guidance with no legal requirement that it is followed, very helpfully stresses: 'This is not a list to be worked through slavishly, but to be selected from as needed for an activity', DfES, Letters and Sounds, (2007b: 48).

Upholding the principles of the Early Years Foundation Stage

We wanted to be sure that we were upholding the principles and framework of the legally enshrined document, *Early Years Foundation Stage* (DfES, 2007a) and in *Continuing the Learning Journey* (QCA, 2005) until children are 7 years old. With this in mind, we developed a set of core nursery rhymes which would introduce children to some of the basic sounds, with a systematic approach in the phonological aspects of learning to read and write. This needed to be done in ways that support the *Early Years Foundation Stage* and continue that learning journey into Key Stage 1 of their primary education.

Singing Mary, Mary Quite Contrary while gardening

Traditional nursery rhymes selected to develop phonemic awareness

Mary, Mary quite contrary

Mary, Mary quite contrary,
How does your garden grow?
With silver bells,
And cockle shells,
And pretty maids all in a row.

Contrasting sounds

Children, as they sing and act out the rhyme, can quickly hear the differences in:

- bells and shells.

Although there are other rhyming words, they are more difficult because of the way they are spaced apart in the rhyme. 'Grow' and 'row' are not as easy for the brain to sort out, so it is best to focus on 'bells' and 'shells'. Using props (bells and shells) makes it easier for children to note the 'b' that goes with the 'bell' and the 'sh' sound that goes with the 'shell'. This is a multi-sensory approach.

In these photographs, there are examples of children becoming involved in some of the sounds of 'Mary, Mary quite contrary'.

- 'b' in bell and 'sh' in shell.

This encourages children to listen to sounds at the beginning of the words, and to hear the difference between the 'b' and the 'sh'.

It is important to talk about the sound at the **beginning of the word** (initial sounds).

- The words rhyme. B-ell and Sh-ell.

This naturally also encourages children to listen to the **rhyme** that sounds the same. It is important to give children the word 'rhyme'.

We found that children responded easily when the sounds were very different at the beginning of the word, and made a good contrast ('b' and 'sh' are in that category).

Children also enjoy the **alliteration** of 'm' in 'Mary, Mary'. Some might even take the word into their vocabulary. If not, it is important to explain that there are the same sounds at the beginning of 'Mary, Mary'.

Humpty Dumpty sat on a wall

Humpty Dumpty had a great fall
All the King's horses and all the King's men
Couldn't put Humpty together again.

In this rhyme, children quickly hear the difference between the 'H' sound in Humpty and the 'D' sound in Dumpty. Once again, there is no emphasis on the written form at this point. Children are given books of nursery rhymes to enjoy, and all the props for singing and acting out the song. They are encouraged to hear the difference in the sounds of the two bits of Humpty Dumpty's name.

In this way, children begin to distinguish between 'm', 'b', 'sh', 'h' and 'd' in these rhymes. They do so through enjoyment of the two nursery rhymes, and encouragement to focus on particular words in the rhymes as they listen to them.

Singing the familiar rhyme helps memory of similar sounds (rhyming chunks) and differences (initial word sounds)

Building Humpty Dumpty's wall

Enjoying the singing and together acting out the nursery rhyme is the most important thing

We are likely to put children off if we over-teach. Over-teaching (Langer, 1997) damages learning. The younger the child, the more the damage that can be done. The aim is to support children's natural delight in rhyme, alliteration and rhythm, and to open up the world of literacy and literature in doing so. 'Pushing a child toward a new skill too soon can cut short the preceding period of organisation and preparation which provides the basis for later automaticisation of functioning' (Goddard-Blythe, 2004: 48).

Alliteration

The children will probably already know the rhyme, 'Peter pointer' by this time. They readily take to listening to the alliteration of the 'p' sound at the beginning of 'Peter' and 'pointer'. So that they have another experience of alliteration, this time contrasting with the 'M' in Mary, Mary! This is a good time to introduce:

Children can enjoy the alliteration of the 's' sound 'See saw'. The rhyme is not highlighted but makes a memorable backcloth which aids phonological awareness

See Saw, Margery Daw

Johnny shall have a new master.
He shall have but a penny a day
Because he can't work any faster.

The importance of not rushing children through their journey into literacy

Before introducing children to stage 2 nursery rhymes through poetry cards, in the next chapter, it is important to ensure that children are not being rushed. After all, when later on a child has grown into an adult and attends an interview for a job, no one is going to ask these questions of the candidate:

- At what age were you toilet trained?
- When did you begin to sleep through the night as a baby?
- At what age did you begin to read and write?

Early is not important. Early is not best. What matters is that the child becomes a life-long reader and writer, a bookworm, and someone who takes pleasure in literature and seeking information and reflecting on thoughts through reading and writing.

Where is each child in their unique journey into literacy?

It is important not to rush children through the important beginnings of their journey into literacy. They cannot continue to travel well if the essentials are not in place. The focus of this book is on time-honoured essentials which have stood the test of time across the world.

'Findings from different research programmes are sometimes contradictory or inconclusive, and often call for further studies to test tentative findings … Schools and settings cannot always wait for the results of long-term research studies' (Rose, 2006: 15). It is always important not to throw out the baby with the bath water. New research findings, as yet not reliable, might indicate a greater emphasis on one aspect or another, depending on the interests of particular researchers, funders and politicians. There is currently a focus on phonic work. The most important thing is, however, that this is deeply embedded within a broad and rich language environment, which enables development and learning indoors and outdoors. The *Early Years Foundation Stage* (DfES, 2007a) emphasizes this, as do the curriculum frameworks in all the UK countries.

Before introducing poetry cards

Before acting on the next chapter, be sure that children are confident and competent in all the aspects below. These connect to the *Early Years Foundation Stage* (DfES, 2007a), which is legally enshrined, and to the seven aspects in phase 1 of *Letters and Sounds* (DfES, 2007b), which is for guidance only.

You will find all these aspects integrated into the *Early Years Foundation Stage*, and they are integrated into the chapters throughout this book.

Aspect 1 – environmental sounds

- Are adults and children spontaneously playing and talking together?
- Exploring sounds that different animals, objects, languages, accents and dialects make, and everyday sounds of life, such as traffic in the street?
- Are you helping children to hear the sounds of different languages and to learn some of the different sounds, such as 'r' in French and 'th' in English, 'g' in Arabic?
- Are adults encouraging language for thinking and feeling?
- Encouraging shoulder and other gross motor movements?
- Making role-play areas? And props for play scenarios?
- Going on listening walks?
- Encouraging quiet listening to sounds around us?

The Gingerbread Man – rhythm and rhyme

- Exploring sounds outdoors and indoors?
- Using musical instruments and making them too?
- Playing games with sounds in them?
- Are you making sure groups are very small? (Eight is a large group, two to four comprise a small group.)
- Using props with sounds in stories and rhymes? (Action songs and nursery rhymes and stories.)

Gradually children will identify what a sound is, and know where it comes from. They will find similar sounds. They will develop language to describe the sounds. They will actively engage with other children in this.

Aspect 2 – Instrumental sounds

Are you doing all of these things?

- Encouraging children to make musical instruments and to talk about the sounds they make?
- Do you use musical instruments indoors and outdoors?
- Which children make patterns of rhythm?
- Is there opportunity for children to revisit adult-led experiences in their own way and choosing, and in their free-flow spontaneous play?
- Do children listen to each other and respond as they play?
- Do you put new words to old familiar songs sometimes?
- Do you give children musical instruments when you sing with them?
- Do you encourage children to know and recognize which sounds different instruments make?
- Do you help children to play loudly and softly, and to follow or lead in playing an instrument?
- Do you make sound effects when you tell stories and rhymes?
- Do you encourage children to 'play' instruments and listen to each other?

You will help the children to increase their vocabulary of sound descriptions, to match a sound to its source, to use sounds imaginatively in rhymes and stories, and to know which sounds they like and dislike.

Aspect 3 – Body percussion

- Are the children spontaneously splashing, stamping and making sounds in the garden with rhythm?

- Are you encouraging rhythm and beat as you sing action songs, nursery rhymes and poetry cards?
- Do children enjoy contrasts in speed and loudness?
- Join in the words and actions?
- Articulate the words easily?
- Keep in time to the beat?
- Imitate the sounds and actions?
- Make up their own patterns of sound?

Children will begin to make up their own stories and rhymes, talk about the sounds they hear and group sounds (as loud and soft, fast and slow).

Making music – rhythm

Aspect 4 – rhythm and rhyme

- Are you helping children to develop a stock of familiar rhymes and poems through hearing them over and over again?
- Are you helping children with disabilities and learning difficulties to access these in ways right for them as unique individuals?
- Are you making sure that children with English as an additional language understand the poetry or rhyme, and are being helped to tune into the rhythm and sound of the English language?
- Are you sharing books with children?
- Are you encouraging children to give alternative words to familiar songs?
- Are you encouraging children to use the ideas from the rhymes, poetry and stories you tell them and read to them in the role-play area and with the story-box props, small world, and so on?
- Do you have books with rhymes in them?
- Do you sing finger rhymes, action songs and nursery rhymes every day?
- Do you point out initial sounds and rhymes in the songs?
- Do you play with words – for example, clapping the syllables in each child's name?

Wiggly wiggly worms – alliteration

Gradually, children will see a pattern in the syllables of words, sing and chant rhyming strings, and recognize when words rhyme. They will join in with making a rhythmic sound, imitate rhythms they hear and keep to the beat. They will make their own rhymes and rhythms.

Aspect 5 – alliteration

- Do you see children enjoying saying things like 'wiggly worms'. Or when you sing and read them rhymes?

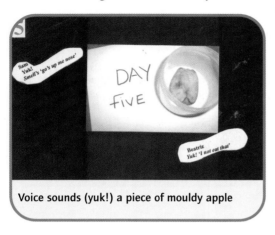

Voice sounds (yuk!) a piece of mouldy apple

- Does the book corner have rhymes with alliteration in them?
- Do you point out initial sounds to children?
- Do they enjoy it when you help them to think of and find words with the same starting sound – for example, when you sing and act the Humpty Dumpty nursery rhyme?
- Are you careful not to exaggerate the sound at the beginning – 'P' not 'puh'?

Aspect 6 – voice sounds

- Do you encourage children to vocalize sounds and make up onomatopoeic ones? Ouch!
- Do they enjoy talking about the sound? 'Yum' when they enjoy eating something is a shorter sound than the long sound in 'oooooooooou!' when they have to swerve to avoid something on their bike.
- Do you tell them rhymes with voice sounds in them?

Aspect 7 – oral blending and segmenting

- Do they engage with the nursery rhymes you have introduced?
- Do they enjoy making a steady beat?
- Do they enjoy the rhyme aspect?
- Do they, with your help, pick out the initial sound 'm' for 'Mary, Mary quite contrary'?

If a child is engaging with all seven aspects within the four principles of the *Early Years Foundation Stage* (a unique child, positive relationships, enabling environments outdoors and indoors, development and learning), then you can think about introducing poetry cards to the children and their parents.

Poetry cards make a bridge for a child. They give children the next steps in their journey into literacy. They support phonic work with a meaningful introduction, which engages the interest and enjoyment of children until they are about 7 years old. They keep children connected and anchored in the essentials of communication, language and literacy.

IN SUMMARY

In this chapter, we have:

- taken a specific focus. A few nursery rhymes have been carefully selected to introduce children to the sounds of the English language in ways which specifically help children to develop phonemic awareness
- continued the pattern throughout the book, in emphasizing that this needs to be located within the broad, rich and deep framework of good early childhood practice, with positive relationships, enabling environments for communication, language and literacy for each child
- reminded ourselves that it is important to bring the rhymes alive for children before introducing them to the children.

Chapter 9

Poetry Cards

Poetry cards come late in the journey into literacy in the *Early Years Foundation Stage*, (they go with children until they are about 7 years old), acting as a bridge into phonic work. They emerge out of all the other experiences in the book, and should be seen as part of the broader context in engaging children in the essentials of literacy (see the audit of what needs to be in place at the end of the previous chapter).

They help small groups (of about 2–4 children,) in very enjoyable and engaging ways, towards becoming lifelong bookworms, avid writers and information seekers, creative artists and performers of dramas. Poetry cards:

- give children appropriate experiences with the alphabetic code, blending and segmenting, and the reversing of these
- help parents to share and enjoy
- help literacy experiences with their children as they borrow poetry cards to take home to make meaning from small, manageable chunks of text
- help children to understand that print represents meaning
- help children with learning difficulties and disabilities to enjoy literature
- are multi-sensory and link holistically with all the areas of development and learning in the *EYFS*
- engage children who have English as an additional language to tune into English through small, manageable chunks of text, rhythmic and musical
- help practitioners to develop their subject knowledge about literacy.

Understanding comes before competence

Children know more than they can tell us. It is important that we help children to become aware of what we might call 'literacy situations' before they are able to be explicit about them. 'Literacy enthusiasts are in danger of narrowing the interpretation of what contributes to school progress, while early childhood educators are in danger of setting literacy aside until children get to school' (Clay, 1998: 12–20).

Dame Marie Clay suggests that opening up the world of literacy to children develops by:

- actively providing opportunities for children to notice literacy events
- observing how children show us their literacy awareness
- seizing opportunities to interact with children as they show us their literacy awareness
- opening up further opportunities for literacy learning (communication, language developments, spontaneous freeflow play developments, reading developments and writing developments).

What are poetry cards?

Poetry cards are carefully chosen, well-known, traditional nursery rhymes. They are first introduced through practical experiences (see Chapter 2) to ensure that children fully understand the vocabulary. A child needs to have made pease porridge/pudding, danced a jig or visited a market before a poetry card is introduced.

We taught children who were ready to use two poetry cards.

Making the poetry card

Write out the poetry card

- The rhyme is written out on a large card (the bigger the better – think pantomime!).
- Make the print large, bold and clear.
- Decide which initial letters to highlight.

Introduce the rhyme

- In a small group (eight is a large group; two to four children make a small group).
- In a quiet corner.

Pease Pudding hot
Pease Pudding cold
Pease Pudding in the pot
9 days old

Pease porridge hot
Pease porridge cold
Pease porridge in the pot
9 days old

Some like it hot
Some like it cold
Some like it in the pot
9 days old

To market
To market
To buy a fat pig
Home again
Home again
Jiggety jig

- Sing the rhyme daily all the way through ('Pease porridge hot').
- When it is familiar and well known, introduce the poetry card.

The rhymes we selected

- **Alliterative** initial sounds "p" in pease porridge.
- Same **initial sound** in second poetry card, pig.
- Introduction to **rhyming strings** pot, hot and pig, jig.
- Can be expanded to longer strings if children are ready.
- **Cvc words**, pot, hot, pig, jig suitable for blending, segmenting and reversing.

We wanted to introduce phoneme and grapheme links which involved some of the sounds of speech children can most easily form. The sounds 'h' and 'p' come early, and are usually articulated in the speech of most 3-years-olds. Having said that, the speech and language therapist who worked with us stressed it is hearing the difference between the sounds that is the most important thing.

Poetry cards make a bridge between language development and reading and writing

They give children who are ready:

- small, manageable chunks of text, at the point in their journey into literacy when they are enthusiastic about engaging with this
- successful experiences, as they begin to pick out letters, recognize words and work out the patterns they naturally seek out and love to find
- alliteration, rhythm, syllabification and rhyming chunks, to which they are more naturally drawn than phonemes
- support, as beginner readers, to make the phoneme/grapheme correspondences crucial to learning to read and write
- simple examples of blending phonemes (the smallest units of sound in English) all through regular words as they read them
- simple examples of segmenting words into their separate phonemes, which helps them to spell words
- simple ways to see that blending and segmenting are reversible processes
- steady rhythm, important for memorizing and word recognition
- repetition, supporting memory, sight and sound co-ordination
- simple rhymes involving a highlighted cvc (consonant, vowel, consonant) word
- rhyming strings easily developed from the key words
- initial letters/sounds easily demonstrated in the key words emphasized
- a systematic, supportive bridge into phonic work. This is appropriate and enjoyable for some children in the *Early Years Foundation Stage* but

mainly for 5–7-year-olds. It covers key points in *Letters and Sounds* (DfES, 2007b) but this is not a mandatory document

- the learning takes place in a richly enabling learning environment with multi-sensory experiences in a meaningful context.

Making human sense of reading and writing

Margaret Donaldson points out that when learning makes 'human sense' to children, they can tackle more difficult ideas. When children are in content-free situations, they cannot bring meaning to what they are asked to do.

Content-free situations mean that children cannot naturally connect with what Margaret Donaldson calls the 'givens' of the task. In this case, the task is a literacy one, of making grapheme/phoneme correspondences, segmenting and blending, and reversing these: 'it is of the essence of these kind of problems that you are required to stick to the given. The problem is to be taken as encapsulated, isolated from the rest of existence' (Donaldson, 1978: 200).

Two things need to be in place if children are going to connect with the 'givens' of the move from phonemic awareness to reading texts and writing:

- Children need rich learning environments which are content-full and not content-free. Poetry cards do this.
- Children need to spend time with adults who know about development and learning as well as the structures and systems that are central to developing literacy. Then they can offer the right help at the right time in the right way.

Recognizing words and understanding what they mean

Gough and Tunmer (1986), influencing the 'Simple approach to reading' in the Rose Review (Rose, 2006), see word recognition as the ability to recognize words presented singly out of context. They argue that the only way that children can do this in the context-free situation, is to use phonic rules. But they also argue that word recognition supports meaning-making, understanding and comprehension.

Jeni Riley (2007: 82) emphasizes the need to bring these together, showing that both speedy and automatic decoding and understanding what the word means are

Word comprehension depends on good language development, discourse proficiency and vocabulary. Linguistic processes contribute to comprehension of talking, listening, reading and writing

important in learning to read and write. 'Practitioners who are aware of the multifacetness of the literacy process are more able to provide a variety of appropriate teaching approaches for their pupils' (Riley, 2007: 83).

Environmental print

At first, children problem-solve their way into texts using the signs and clues they find in the context, such as the rhymes in familiar and regularly used poetry cards. This gives them confidence and shows them strategies which are useful in the early stages of engaging with text. Poetry cards help adults to help children learn the strategies that will help them into later phonic work, so that they can have a go at words whether or not they are in a context.

There is not often the need to read a single word out of context in real life. 'EXIT' or 'TOILET' signs are examples, but often environmental print carries captions, 'THIS WAY TO THE MUSEUM'. The context prevents isolation of the words and helps the emergent and beginner reader to recognize and understand particular words. 'Effective word recognition encompasses the ability to read words in and out of context' (Riley, 2007: 84).

Print with a meaningful context 'Hang up your coat'

The child's name

The letters that children learn most readily are those imbued with meaning.

A form of print likely to elicit letter processing is that of personal names. Bloodgood (1999) studied 3–5 year olds. Although the youngest children knew only a few letters and could read few if any preprimer words, they could recognize their own names in isolation and sometimes names of their classmates. Children's comments suggested that initial letters were the salient cues remembered. Also, knowledge of the letters in their own names accounted for most of the letters they could identify. (Ehri, in Snowling and Hulme, 2007: 141)

Much loved poetry cards also help children to engage with texts in meaningful ways.

Using natural learning as a bridge into less natural learning

Showing very young children words and letters in isolation isolates them from context. Poetry cards allow children to bring linguistic meaning to the text through alliteration, rhyme and rhythm, which is a natural process for them. They open the way for them to engage with the 'givens' (phonic work), which are less natural for

We have looked at the importance of the child's name, and other special words throughout the book

the human brain (Carter, 1999: 153). Marian Whitehead (2007: 53) warns against concentration on the 'surface bits' such as correct letter formation or reciting sounds of letters, which neglect, she argues, the real literacy basics. It is important not to undermine what she calls, 'home literacies and meaningful engagements with books and literature'.

Sue Palmer and Ros Bayley emphasize this in their seven strands making the *Foundations of Literacy*: 'The importance of language in education cannot be exaggerated. It is the bedrock on which all formal learning is based, not least the learning of literacy skills' (2004: 7).

The strands they identify as appropriate for 3–6-year-olds, which fit comfortably with this book, are:

- Learning to listen
- Time to talk
- Music, movement and memory
- Storytime
- Learning about print
- Tuning into sound
- Moving into writing.

'Pushing a child toward a new skill too soon can cut short the preceding period of organisation and preparation, which provides the basis for later automatisation of functioning' (Goddard-Blythe, 2004: 48).

Poetry cards are an opportunity for children to engage in discussion about text and also about literature. The story of leaving porridge for nine days is riveting and shocking as the smells and slime grow! Making pease porridge with the children, tasting it, chatting about it and then leaving it for nine days is a major experience.

There were lively discussions in the group of practitioners on training days about whether it should be called pease pudding or pease porridge. For northerners there was no doubt it was pudding. Southerners insist it is porridge.

In what order should children be introduced to the linking of sounds with letters?

The alphabetic principle, all experts agree, is important in the learning of reading and writing. It involves the linking of sounds and letters so that children learn about the way that the smallest units of sound (phonemes) map onto letters in words. The letters might be single ones (pot, p-o-t; hot, h-o-t), or clusters (bell, b-e-ll; shell, sh-e-ll). They are called graphemes.

Some children will, with help, begin to enjoy blending and segmenting words. This means that when they pick out a word like 'hot' on a poetry card, they can blend the sounds h-o-t in order to say 'hot'. They can say a word like 'pot' and write down or find letters for each sound to make the word. On the whole this phase is best matched with children aged 6 and 7 years. However, there will be a significant minority of children who are not yet able to use these strategies. They may have:

- a learning difficulty
- a disability
- be a new arrival in England and new to the sounds of the English language
- have experienced physical and emotional abuse, and so need experiences that open up communication, language and play, with pleasure in being read to by a summer-born child
- simply need more time, (which in most parts of the world is the norm).

English is one of the most irregular and inconsistent languages in the world

In other languages than English (Goswami, 2005), it often makes sense to teach children to read and write with an emphasis on synthetic phonics. Some languages are phonologically consistent, with consonant-vowel (CV) syllable structure (for example Italian, Spanish and Chinese). In some languages a letter or letter cluster is always pronounced in the same way (Italian, Spanish and Greek). Some languages have consistency in the spellings of the written language (Italian). Italian is consistent in all these respects.

It seems natural, in the light of this, that the pioneer educator Maria Montessori argued for synthetic phonics as the prime approach to teaching children to read and write. She was Italian.

The human brain seeks patterns through which it makes sense of chaos

It is always a good idea to go with what the brain finds easiest, building on what children naturally find they can do. As we have seen earlier in the book, the human brain is wired for seeking meaning through finding patterns in the environment.

But Goswami (2005: 274) points out that: 'English is an exceptionally inconsistent alphabetic language because it suffers from a large amount of inconsistency in both reading and writing.' There is less irregularity with rhyming chunks than with phonemes. This means that children can supplement, she argues, mapping sounds to letters (phonemes to graphemes) with recognition of letter patterns they find in rhymes. Poetry cards give children the repetition of a few carefully selected rhymes which allow this to happen. Children will still need to learn what are often called the 'tricky' words as whole words (choir, yacht, people).

'English is a capricious orthography (the written down aspects) in general, but it is much less predictable at the level of the single letter than groups of letters' (Goswami, 2005: 276). Children naturally look at initial and end sounds before paying attention to the middle of words.

Initial sounds

We taught the children the initial sounds so that they would learn the strategies needed to do this.

Because we used only two carefully chosen rhymes, we regularly repeated the rhyming chunks with the children. We displayed the rhyme so that children's attention was drawn to the look of the patterns which occur in the look of the words that rhymed. We used this as background support to the teaching of the initial grapheme/phoneme correspondences, but only if appropriate for individual children.

This process is appropriate for children mainly in Key Stage 1. For a few younger children we could show how to segment and blend and reverse these in relation to 'p' and 'h' with 'hot' and 'pot'. In the second poetry card we introduced 'pig' and 'jig'. We found the children used the rhyme to help them.

The importance of a rich learning environment

The emphasis in the *Early Years Foundation Stage* on a rich, multi-sensory language environment means that children are encouraged in a variety of ways to tune into the sounds of English. The poetry cards provide a supportive backcloth, which helps children to map the sounds (phonemes) onto the graphemes, supported by alliteration, initial sounds and rhyming chunks. Using poetry cards avoids drilling children, and makes this an enjoyable, comfortable experience with literacy. It enriches a child's understanding and engagement with literature. This encourages the systematic teaching of GPC (Grapheme/phoneme correspondence) rules and phoneme segmentation and blending against a backcloth of rich language and the supportive sound patterns of rhyme. But it does not neglect the uniqueness of each child.

These three approaches are important in using the poetry cards:

- Alongside this use alliteration and rhyming chunks so that children actively seek out the patterns in letters and sounds of words, a process which comes naturally to them. Alliteration encourages children to work through the word from left to right.
- Encourage children in what they naturally do, in looking at initial sounds and rhyming chunks, but show them how to blend and segment regular CVC words.
- Help children with the 'tricky' words which just have to be learnt as a whole as sight vocabulary (for example, choir, yacht).

'Run, run as fast as you can
You can't catch me, I'm the gingerbread man'

Children who have learned to listen to the sounds in words get more out of rhymes. This in turn feeds into their possibility to enjoy rhyming strings, and to segment and blend. It is a virtuous circle. But *don't* rush children.

Make sure you know the technical literacy jargon

Jargon often excludes people, so it is important that you try to feel comfortable with recently introduced literacy jargon, and can find ways to share it with parents in an accessible way. It is very unfortunate that in the past decade the language has become so technical. It is sad to think that the development of communication, language and literacy could be hampered because practitioners and parents, and grandparents, are required to develop unfamiliar vocabulary around such an important aspect of children's development and learning.

Explaining something in simple words is a very good way of making sure you really understand it. If you cannot explain to a colleague, parent or carer the meaning of 'phoneme', 'grapheme', 'blending' and 'segmenting', then you do not understand the subject matter. If you do not understand, you should not introduce poetry cards to children. It might do more damage than good.

Phoneme　The smallest unit of sound in a word.

Grapheme　The letter or cluster of letters representing a sound.

GPC　Grapheme/phoneme correspondence.

Alphabetic principle　This is about the way sounds and letters link. Sounds can be represented by writing one of the 26 letters of the alphabet, or by a cluster of letters. Because there are 44 sounds in the English language, there are not enough letters to represent each sound. All experts agree that it is important for children to understand the links between letters and sounds.

Synthetic phonics　This is one kind of phonics. It is based on the belief that reading is a simple matter of decoding and encoding. It emphasizes the regular words, describing those that do not follow the rules as 'tricky' words. These have to be learnt as '**sight vocabulary**'.

Segmenting　This involves separating out the sounds in a word that is regular.

Blending　This involves building the separate sounds up into a word in order, all through the word. It is useful for regular words.

Syllable　This is part of a word which is pronounced as one beat. For example, porridge is two syllables (two beats) in the rhyme 'Pease porridge hot'. Clapping the beat of children's names is a popular way for children to enjoy working out the number of syllables in a word.

CVC words   Consonant, vowel, consonant.

Rhyming chunks   Pig, jig, in 'To market, to market, to buy a fat pig'.

Analytic phonics   This approach to phonics helps children to look for patterns in words which have larger chunks than phonemes.

Why introduce one poetry card rather than another?

It is important to think carefully why a particular poetry card should be introduced. With the introduction of nursery rhymes, in the last chapter, the emphasis was on the sounds of alliteration, rhythm and rhyme. The emphasis is different with the introduction of poetry cards. The rhyming words emphasized must SOUND and LOOK the same (be spelt in the same way) if they are to be helpful.

> Doctor Foster
> Went to Gloucester
> In a shower of rain.
> He stepped in a puddle
> Right up to his middle
> And never went there again.

The sounds and look are not the same in this rhyme. This would not make a good poetry card.

Using the poetry card 'Pease porridge hot'

- Children are naturally drawn to enjoying rhyming chunks. It is hard to stop them from finding these patterns in the words once they have been introduced to them, providing they are repeated often enough.
- You will find yourself able to discuss alliteration (pease porridge). Children are naturally drawn to alliteration, and once found they are fascinated and delight in it.
- Rhyming strings are part of the essentials of literacy, and are a strong component of poetry cards (hot, pot, got, lot, dot, jot).
- Chukovsky (1963) and the Opies (1988) were famous for their work in gathering

It is important for children to build an understanding that print represents the symbols which carry meaning, and can be read. It is also important that they approach print with developing sensitivity to the way sounds are mapped onto it

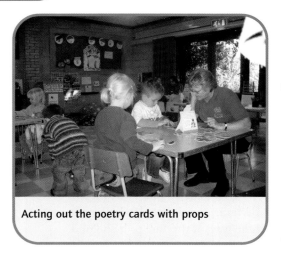

Acting out the poetry cards with props

examples of the joy children take in nonsense rhymes of their own making. Children need to know rhymes in order to make their own.

- Encourage the children to predict the next word. Discuss why they are right, and how they came to that decision – because it rhymes … because the sound is 'p' and then 'o' and than 't', so it says 'pot', and so on. In this way, children develop the language of literacy, which will help them to appreciate literature too.

We emphasized 'hot' and 'pot'.

- These were the last words in the line.
- We were careful to articulate the sounds clearly for the children, (as we had done in singing the oral and aural nursery rhymes – see Chapter 7) p-o-t (not puh-oh-tuh).
- We selected these words because they have three phonemes, with a single syllable, and they rhyme.
- We segmented, and children joined in if they wished or could.
- Pick out the initial **grapheme** you have selected (for example, 'p' in 'pot'). Link this with children's names **of the same letter**.
- This should be at the end of the line.
- Give children the name of the sound it makes in this situation. It is important to say the sound correctly. For example, 'p' or 'h' without putting an extra 'uh' sound on the end (for example, 'P' as in 'Patrick', 'Parvel').
- Having introduced the **sounds** in the initial letters of words 'p' in '**p**ot' and 'h' in '**h**ot', on another day, pick out rhyming words, such as 'hot' and 'pot' in the rhyme 'Pease porridge hot'. 'Pot' and 'hot' are cvc words. (consonant, vowel, consonant). Children are not naturally drawn to doing this and will usually be attracted, instead, by the initial sound and the rhyming chunk. Poetry cards give an embedded context that makes 'human sense' to them. But they also keep pressure from children if they are not ready for this. They can enjoy the rhyme story and characters, which engages them with literature (hopefully for life).

Poetry cards give children anchor points

Children begin to pick out letters/graphemes they know

By the time the children are introduced to the second poetry card, they may well be beginning to pick out letters they know, such as 'p' and 'h'.

Children begin to pick out rhyming chunks they find

They begin to see what the 'p' says, and what the 'j' says in 'pig' and 'jig'. As Karmiloff-Smith (1992) notes, children are both problem-solvers and problem-generators. They revel in both, and are definitely not just passive receivers of what we teach them. They are active learners, using us as anchors, guides and resources.

They like the idea that you can break up words and then make them again

Some children will be able to segment the words 'pot' and 'hot' into their sounds, and blend the sounds 'p', 'h', 'o' and 't' into the words 'pot' and 'hot'. They can see that they can be reversed too. However, in order to do this, children must understand the relationship between parts and whole. This is usually established by the age of 6 or 7 years.

They begin to see that words stand for things

The picture of the pig, on the poetry card, will help them to remember that pig begins with a 'p'. Having picture cards, word cards and letter cards to go with the poetry card is very helpful too. Captions can also be helpful having one line of the poetry card on a strip of card helps children to pick out the words. Children will often seek out different aspects to focus on as they engage spontaneously with these play props.

They begin to realize that you need connecting words

As they play with the words from the poetry card, they have some left over which do not go with pictures in the way 'pot' goes with the picture of the pot. These words are 'and', 'to' and so on. They are what Ragnarsdottir calls connecting words.

Children begin spontaneously to choose to play with the words and props around the poetry cards

In this book, many examples are given of ways to enhance the processes of literacy. The mark-making area is invaluable in this way. So are the many games children enjoy using written words in ways which connect with the poetry cards. Sets of alphabets give other children great satisfaction, and give them opportunities to blend and segment words. Sharing books and picking out interesting things to say about the text fascinates others. It is very important that the indoor and outdoor learning environments open up different aspects of the world of communication, language and literacy in a huge variety of ways.

Given that each child is unique, it goes without saying that children will respond and engage with these in their own way (Ellis, 2007). What is important is that they can find ways which are right for them, and get the help they need when they need it.

Environmental print

Encourage spontaneous opportunities for children to follow through on the essentials of literacy through poetry cards

- Leave the props around for children to use with the rhyme.
- Make full use of everyday experiences to raise the children's awareness, and to help them make links. They will soon begin to pick out letters in their name, or letters at the beginning of words on the poetry card, and to say the sounds. Opportunities arise in the garden, at toilet and snack times, at the computer, during group times, and when looking at environmental print and sharing stories.
- Make a rhyme box with the children. In an earlier chapter, we looked at the importance of pattern and how it helps the brain to make sense of many aspects of life, including reading and writing. Children love to see the patterns in rhyme, and appreciate adults who help them to do this.

There is a wealth of research (including classic studies by Blakemore and Frith, 2005; Clay, 1998; Goddard-Blythe, 2004; Goswami, 2007; Snowling and Hulme, 2007) which points to reading and writing being complex processes in development and learning, involving the use by the brain of integrating strategies. Don Holdaway (1979: 97), a pioneer of the teaching of reading and writing, suggests that, 'Separate skills taught separately tend to be used separately by children.' The *Early Years Foundation Stage* sets children off to a rich, broad and deep start (Hall, 2007) with the essentials of communication, language and literacy. It is crucial that this continues until 7 years of age.

Poetry cards are a bridge into the next part of the journey into literacy

Paving the way for phonic work is only 1 per cent of the *Early Years Foundation Stage*. Using a poetry card with children is so much more than phonics. Poetry cards help us to give children some very crucial essentials for learning to read and write.

Poetry cards bridge the move from phonemic awareness to the alphabetic principle of mapping sounds onto letters and clusters of letters. They are therefore very useful in the first years of statutory schooling until children are 7 years old.

IN SUMMARY

Poetry cards need careful introduction if they are to engage a diverse range of children, but the effort of introducing them in ways right for each unique child brings reward.

- Seeing the poetry cards that adults have made encourages children to make their own cards, and to have a go at writing.
- They give children an important part of the time-honoured canon of literature in English culture, helping them to tune into the sounds, rhythms and cadences of the English language which are essential to fluent reading and writing.
- The literary themes of the poems chosen are cross-cultural (eating, falling down, tending growing plants, and so on).
- Poetry cards, in important ways, offer children the technical help they need in order to read and write in English.
- They help children to link with other areas of development and learning: 'All areas of development and learning are connected to one another and are equally important' (DfES, EYFS, 2007a:)
- Poetry cards are resonant with the principles of the *EYFS*. They focus on the unique child, encourage positive relationships, create enabling environments outdoors and indoors, and value developing learning.
- In this book, we have embraced the complexities of helping children on their journey into language and literacy. The essentials of literacy begin with a baby's early communications with us. We will see these come to fruition at the end of the first 6 or 7 years, as children communicate with and without words, and begin to read and write in ways which are right for them, for the rest of their lives.

Bibliography

Abbott, L. and Langston, A. (eds) (2006) *Parents Matter*. Maidenhead: Open University Press/McGraw-Hill.

Adams, M. (1990) *Beginning to Read: Thinking and Learning about Print*. Cambridge, MA: MIT Press.

Ashton-Warner, S. (1965) *Teacher*. New York: Simon & Schuster.

Baddeley, P. and Eddershaw, C. (1994) *Not so Simple Picture Books: Developing Responses to Literature with 4–12 Year Olds*. Stoke-on-Trent: Trentham.

Barber, M. (see Stannard and Huxford).

Bartholomew, L. and Bruce, T. (1993) *Getting to Know You: A Guide to Record-Keeping in Early Childhood Education*, London: Hodder & Stoughton.

Basic Skills Agency (BSA) (2005) *Language and Play*. London: BSA.

Bateson, G. (1995, 1976) 'A theory of play and fantasy', in J. Bruner, A. Jolly and K. Sylva (eds) *Play: Its Role in Development and Evolution*. New York: Basic Books.

Bialystok, E. (1991) 'Letters, sounds and symbols: changes in children's understanding of written language', *Applied Psycholinguistics*, 12: 75–89.

Bissex, G. (1980) *GYNS AT WRK (GENIUS AT WORK: A child learns to write and read)*. Cambridge, MA: MIT Press.

Blakemore, C. (2001) 'What makes a developmentally appropriate early childhood curriculum?', lecture given at the Royal Society of Arts, 14 February.

Blakemore, S.J. and Frith, U. (2005) *The Learning Brain: Lessons for Education*. Oxford: Blackwell.

Bloodgood, J. (1999) 'What's in a name? Children's name writing and name acquisition'. *Reading Research Quarterly*, 34: 342–67.

Bradley, L. and Bryant, P. (1988) 'Rhyme and reason in reading and spelling', International Academy for Research in Learning Difficulties, monograph series, no. 1. Ann Arbor, MI: University of Michigan Press.

Britton, J. (1970) *Language and Learning*. London: Allen Lane.

Brown, G. (2007) *The Mansion House Speech*, City Hall, London, 20 June.

Browne, A. (2001) *Developing Language and Literacy 3–8*. 2nd edn. London: Paul Chapman Publishing.

Bruce, T. (1991) *Time to Play in Early Childhood Education and Care*. London: Hodder & Stoughton.

Bruce, T. (2001) *Learning Through Play: Babies, Toddlers and the Foundation Years*. London: Hodder/Arnold.

Bruce, T. (2004a) *Cultivating Creativity: Babies, Toddlers and the Early Years*. London: Hodder/Arnold.

Bruce, T. (2004b) *Developing Learning in Early Childhood*. London: Paul Chapman Publishing.

Bruce, T. (2005a) 'Editor's notes', *Early Childhood Practice: The Journal for Multi-Professional Partnerships*, 7: 17–20.

Bruce, T. (2005b) *Early Childhood Education*. 3rd edn. London: Hodder/Arnold.

Bruce, T. and Meggitt, C. (2007) *Childcare and Education*. 5th edn. London: Hodder/Arnold.

Bruner, J. (1977) *The Process of Education*. 2nd edn. Cambridge, MA, and London: Harvard University Press.

Bryant, P. and Bradley, L. (1985) *Children's Reading Problems*. Oxford: Blackwell.

Buckley, B. (2003) *Children's Communication Skills from Birth to Five Years*. Abingdon: Routledge.

Bullock, A. (1975) A Language for life: The Bullock Report. HMSO: London.

Carter, R. (1999) *Mapping the Mind*. London: Seven Dials, Orion.

Chukovsky, K. (1963) *From Two to Five*. Berkeley, CA: University of California Press.

Clarke, M. (1976) *Young Fluent Readers: What Can They Teach Us?* London: Heinemann.

Clay, M. (1975) *What Did I Write?* London: Heinemann.

Clay, M. (1982) *Observing Young Readers – Selected Readings*. Portsmouth, NH: Heinemann.

Clay, M. (1986) *Reading: The Patterning of Complex Behaviour*. 3rd edn. Auckland: Heinemann.

Clay, M. (1993) *An Observational Survey of Early Literacy Development*. Portsmouth, NH: Heinemann.

Clay, M. (1998) 'From Acts to Awareness in Early Literacy', *Children's Issues*, 2(1): 12–20.

Coltheart, M. (2007) 'Modeling reading: the dual-route approach', in M. Snowling and C. Hulme (eds), *The Science of Reading*. Oxford, Malden, MA and Carlton, Victoria: Blackwell.

Creating the Picture only available on the web. This can be downloaded from http://www.standards.dcsf.gov.uk/primary.publications/foundation_stage/creating-picture/The reference is: 00283-2007DWO-EN-01.

Crystal, D. (2006) *Words, Words, Words*. Oxford: Oxford University Press.

Damasio, A. (2004) *Looking for Spinoza*. London: Random Press.

Department for Education and Employment (DfEE) (1997) *The Implementation of the National Literacy Strategy: Final Report*, London: Department for Education and Employment.

Department for Education and Employment (DfEE) (1998) *The National Literacy Strategy: Framework for Teaching*. London: DfEE.

Department for Education and Skills (DfES) (2004) *Playing with Sounds*. London: DfES.

Department for Education and Skills (DfES) (2005a) *Communicating Matters: The Strands of Communication and Language*. London: DfES.

Department for Education and Skills (DfES) (2005b) *Early Reading Development Pilot – Consultant File*. London: DfES.

Department for Education and Skills (DfES) (2006a) *Independent Review of the Teaching of Reading: Final Report*. Nottingham: DfES. Crown Copyright.

Department for Education and Skills (DfES) (Togerson, C.J., Brooks, G. and Hall, J.) (2006c) *A Systematic Review of the Research Literature on the Use of Phonics in the Teaching of Reading and spelling*. London: DfES.

Department for Education and Skills (DfES) (2006b) *Seamless Transitions – Supporting Continuity in Young Children's Learning*. London: DfES.

Department for Education and Skills (DfES) (2007a) *Early Years Foundation Stage*. London: DfES.

Department for Education and Skills (DfES) (2007b) *Letters and Sounds: Principles and Practice of High Quality Phonics*. London: DfES.

Department for Education and Skills (DfES) (2007c) 'Creating the Picture', only available on the web: www.standards.dcsf.gov.uk/primary/publications/foundation_stage/creating_picture/.Reference: 00283-2007DWO-EN-01.

Department for Education and Skills/Qualifications and Curriculum Authority (DfES/QCA) (2000) *Curriculum Guidance for the Foundation Stage*. London: DfES.

Department for Education and Skills/Qualifications and Curriculum Authority (DfES/QCA) (2003) *Foundation Stage Profile Handbook*. London: DfES.

Dombey, H. (2006) 'How should we teach children to read?', *Books for Keeps*, 156: 6–7.

Donaldson, M. (1978) *Children's Minds*. London: Fontana/Collins.

Dunn, O. (2007) Books for Birth to Threes, *Nursery World*, June.

Dunne, J. (1988) *The Beginnings of Social Understanding*. Oxford: Blackwell.

Edgington, M. (2004) *The Foundation Teacher in Action: Teaching 3, 4 and 5 Year Olds*. 3rd edn. London: Paul Chapman Publishing/Sage.

Edwards, C., Gandini, L. and Forman, G. (1998) *The Hundred languages of Children*. Westport, CT and London: Ablex Publishing.

Ehri, L. (2007) 'Development of sight word reading: phases and findings', in M. Snowling and C. Hulme (eds), *The Science of Reading*. Oxford, Malden, MA and Carlton, Victoria: Blackwell.

Ellis, M. (1992) 'Tempo perception and performance of elementary students in grades 3–6', *Journal of Research in Music Education*, 40(41): 329–41.

Ellis, S. (2006) 'A response to Stuart', *The Psychology of Education Review*, 30(2): 21–2.

Featherstone, S. (ed.) (2006) *L is for Sheep: Getting Ready for Phonics*. Lutterworth: Featherstone Education.

Ferreiro, E. (1997) 'Writing and thinking about writing systems', *Conference Lectures on Literacy: From Research to Practice*. London: Institute of Education.

Feynman, R. (1990) *What Do You Care What Other People Think? Further Adventures of a Curious Character*. London: Unwin Hyman.

Frabetti, R. (2005) 'Eyes and silences', *Early Childhood Practice: The Journal for Multi-Professional Partnerships*, 7(1): 63–72.

Froebel, F. (1887) *The Education of Man*. New York: Appleton.

Goddard-Blythe, S. (2004) *The Well-Balanced Child – Movement and Early Learning*. Stroud: Hawthorn Press.

Goswami, U. (1998) *Cognition in Children*. Hove: Psychology Press Ltd.

Goswami, U. (2005) 'Synthetic phonics and learning to read: a cross-cultural perspective', *Educational Psychology in Practice*, 21(4): 273–82.

Goswami, U. (2006) 'Research evidence and teaching phonics: a response to Stuart', *The Psychology of Education Review*, 30(2): 23–5.

Goswami, U. and Bryant, P. (1990) *Phonological Skills and Learning to Read*. Hove: Psychology Press.

Goswami, U. and Ziegler, J.C. (2006) 'A developmental perspective on the neural code for written words', *Trends in Cognitive Sciences*, 10(4): 142–3.

Gough, P. and Tunmer, W. (1986) 'Decoding, reading and reading disability', *Remedial and Special Education*, 7: 6–10.

Greenland, P. (2000) *Hopping Home Backwards: Body Intelligence and Movement Play*. Leeds: Jabadao/Reading.

Greenland, P. (2006) 'Physical Development' in *Early Childhood: A Guide for Students*, T. Bruce (ed.). London: Sage.

Griffiths, N. (2001) *Storysacks*. Reading and Language Information Centre, University of Reading.

Hall, K. (2007) 'Rose in context: the teaching of reading in initial teacher education', keynote address at the Conference of the Universities Council for the Education of Teachers (UCET), London, 11 September.

Hall, N. and Robinson, A. (1996) *Learning about Punctuation*. Clevedon, PA and Adelaide: Multilingual Matters.

Harrison, E. (1895) *A Study of Child Nature from the Kindergarten Standpoint*. New York and London: Garland. Originally published by The Chicago Kindergarten College in 1895.

Holdaway, D. (1979) *Foundations of Literacy*. London: Scholastic.

Hutchin, V. (2006) 'Meeting Individual Needs', in T. Bruce, *Early Childhood: A Guide for Students*. London: Sage.

Johnson, R. and Watson, J. (2005) 'The effects of synthetic phonics teaching of reading and spelling attainment: a seven year longitudinal study', www.scotland.gov.uk/Resource/Doc/36496/0023582.pdf.

Kalliala, M. (2005) *Play Culture in a Changing World*, Maidenhead: Open University Press. McGraw-Hill.

Karmiloff-Smith, A. (1992) *Beyond Modularity: A Developmental Perspective on Cognitive Science*. Cambridge, MA: MIT Press/Bradford Books.

Kuhlman, K. and Schweinhart, L. (1999) *Movement, Music and Timing*. Ypsilanti, MI: High Scope Educational Research Foundation.

Laevers, F. (1994) *The Innovative Project 'Experiential Education' and the Definition of Quality in Education*. Leuven: Katholieke Universiteit.

Langer, E. (1997) *The Power of Mindful Learning*. Harlow: Addison-Wesley.

Liebschner, J. (1992) *A Child's World: Freedom and Guidance in Froebel's Theory and Practice*. Oxford: Butterworth Press.

Lilley, J. (1967) *Friedrich Froebel: A Selection from his Writings*. Cambridge: Cambridge University Press.

MacIntyre, C. and McVitty, K. (2004) *Movement and Learning in the Early Years*. London: Paul Chapman Publishing.

Makin, L. and Whitehead, M. (2004) *How to Develop Children's Early Literacy: A Guide for Carers and Educators*. London: Paul Chapman Publishing.

Mallett, M. (2005) *The Primary English Encyclopaedia: The Heart of the Curriculum*. London: Fulton.

Marsh, J. and Hallett, E. (eds) (1999) *Desirable Literacies: Approaches to Language and Literacy in the Early Years*. London: Paul Chapman Publishing.

Matthews, J. (2003) *Drawing and Painting: Children and Visual Representation*. 2nd edn. London: Paul Chapman Publishing.

Meade, A. (2003) 'What are the implications of brain studies on early childhood education?', *Early Childhood Practice: The Journal for Multi-Professional Partnerships*, 5(2): 4–18.

Meek, M. (1982) *Learning to Read*. London, Sydney and Toronto: Bodley Head.

Meek, M., Warlow, G. and Barton, G. (1977) *The Cool Web: The Pattern of Children's Reading*. London, Sydney and Toronto: Bodley Head.

Montessori, M. (1912) *The Montessori Method*. London: Heinemann.

Murray, L. and Andrews, L. (2000) *The Social Baby*. Richmond: CP Publishing.

National Institute of Child Health and Human Development (2002) *Report of the National Reading Panel, Teaching Children to Read: An Evidence-based Assessment of the Scientific Research Literature on Reading and its Implications for Reading Instruction*. Washington, DC: US Government Printing Office.

Nawrotzki, K. (2006) 'Froebel is Dead: Long Live Froebel!', *History of Education*, 35(2): 209–23.

Nutbrown, C., Hannon, P. and Morgan, A. (2005) *Early Literacy Work with Families: Policy, Practice and Research*. London: Sage.

Ockelford, A. (1996) *All Join In: A Framework for Making Music with Children and Young People Who Are Visually Impaired and Have Learning Difficulties*. Peterborough: RNIB.

Opie, I. and Opie, P. (1988) *The Singing Game*. Oxford and New York: Oxford Unviersity Press.

Ouvry, M. (2004) *Sounds Like Playing: Music in the Early Years Curriculum*. London: BAECE.

Palmer, S. and Bayley, R. (2004) *Foundations of Literacy: A balanced Approach to Language, Listening and Literacy Skills in the Early Years*. Stafford: Network Educational Press.

Papousek, H. and Papousek, M. (1987) 'Intuitive parenting: a dialectic counterpart to the infant's integrative competence', in J. Osofsky (ed.), *Handbook of Infant Development*. 2nd edn. New York: Wiley.

Pascal, C. and Bertram, T. (2006) *Connectedness, Exploration and Meaning Making, BEEL Project*, Birmingham: CREC (Centre for Research in Early Childhood).

Piaget, J. (1962) *Play, Dreams and Imitation in Childhood*. London: Routledge and Kegan Paul.

Pinker, S. (1999) *Words and Rules*. New York: Basic Books.

Poulsson, E. (1921) *Finger Plays for Nursery and Kindergarten*. Norwood, MA: Norwood Press. Originally printed in Boston in 1893 by Lothrop, Lee and Shepard Co.

Qualifications and Curriculum Authority (QCA) (2005) *Continuing the Learning Journey (From Foundation Stage into Key Stage 1)*. London: QCA.

Ragnarsdottir, H. (2006) 'Constructing the tools for participation in culture and democracy: children's language proficiency at age 5½ and the implications of individual variation', EECERA Conference, Reykjavik, 1 September.

Riley, J. (1999) *Teaching Reading at Key Stage 1 and Before*. Cheltenham: Stanley Thornes.

Riley, J. (2006) *Language and Literacy 3–7*. London: Sage.

Riley, J. (2007) *Learning in the Early Years: 3–7*. 2nd edn. London: Sage.

Rose, J. (2006) *Independent Review of the Teaching of Early Reading*. Nottingham: DfES.

Rose, J. (2006) *Independent Review of the Teaching of Early Reading: Final Report*. London: Department of Education and Skills.

Siraj-Blatchford, I., Sylva, K., Muttock, S., Gilden, R. and Bell, D. (2002) *Researching Effective Pedagogy in the Early Years*, DfES Research Report No. 356, Norwich, HMSO.

Siraj-Blatchford, I. (2006) Conference paper presented on the findings of REPEY project at Children's Centres – improving outcomes for young children through integrated services, London: 14 December.

Snow, C. and Juel, C. 'Teaching children to read: what do we know about how to do it?', in M. Snowling and C. Hulme (eds), *The Science of Reading*. Oxford, Malden, MA and Carlton, Victoria: Blackwell.

Snowling, M. and Hulme, C. (2007) *The Science of Reading*. Oxford, Malden, MA and Carlton, Victoria: Blackwell.

Spencer, B., Bruce, T. and Dowling, M. (2007) 'A real achievement', *Nursery World*, 5 July: 10–11.

Spratt, J. (2006) 'Practical Projects: Birth to 5 Years', in T. Bruce (ed.), *Early Childhood: A Guide for Students*. London: Sage.

Spratt, J. (2007) Finger rhymes: why are they important?', *Early Childhood Practice: The Journal for Multi-Professional Partnerships*, 9(1): 43–54.

Stannard, J. and Huxford, L. (2007) *The Literacy Game*. Abingdon and New York: Routledge.

Stanovich, K. (2000) *Progress in Understanding Reading*. New York: Guilford Press.

Stuart, M. (2006) *Learning to Read: A Professorial Lecture*. London: Institute of Education

Styles, M. and Bearne, E. (2003) *Art, Narrative and Childhood*. Stoke-on-Trent, UK and Sterling, USA: Trentham.

Trevarthen, C. (1999–2000) *Musicality and the Intrinsic Motive Pulse: Evidence from Human Psychobiology and Infant Communication*, Special Issue of *Music Scientiae, Rhythm, Musical Narrative and Origins of Human Communication*: 156–99.

Trevarthen, C. (2004) 'Learning about ourselves from children: why a growing human brain needs interesting companions', Perceptions-in-action laboratories: University of Edinburgh.

Trevarthen, C. and Aitken, A. (2001) 'Infant intersubjectivity: research, theory and clinical applications', *Journal of Child Psychiatry*, 42(1): 3–48.

United Kingdom Literacy Association (UKLA) (2005) *Submission to the Review of Best Practice in the Teaching of Early Reading*. Royston: UKLA.

Vygotsky, L. (1978) *Mind in Society: The Development of Higher Psychological Processes*. Cambridge, MA: Harvard University Press.

Whitehead, M. (1999) *Supporting Language and Literacy Development in the Early Years*. Buckingham, and Philadelphia, PA: Open University Press.

Whitehead, M. (2004) *Language and Literacy in the Early Years*. 3rd edn. London: Sage.

Whitehead, M. (2007) *Developing Language and Literacy with Young Children*. 3rd edn. London: Paul Chapman Publishing.

Wyse, D. (2003) 'The National Literacy Strategy: a critical review of empirical evidence', *British Journal of Research Journal*, 29(6): 903–16.

Wyse, D. and Styles, M. (2007) *Synthetic phonics and the teaching of reading: the debate surrounding England's Rose Review*. Oxford: Blackwell.

Ziegler, J.C. and Goswami, U. (2006) 'Becoming literate in different languages: similar problems, different solutions', *Developmental Science*, 9(5): 429–53.

Index

Food and Health in Early Childhood

Deborah Albon & Penny Mukherji

London Metropolitan University

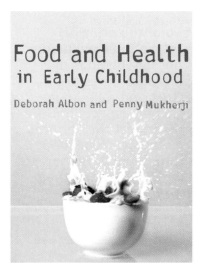

`This highly readable, thoroughly researched book explores food and eating in an historical, cultural and psychological context and, as public concern about children's nutrition rises, its publication is timely. Food and Health in Early Childhood is a comprehensive, clearly written text enriched with case studies and pertinent reflective activities to consolidate learning' - **Angela Underdown, Associate Professor, Early Childhood Studies, University of Warwick**

Contents

Policy Development / Nutrition, Health and Development / Healthy Eating Guidelines / Health Inequalities / Food, Eating and Emotion / Food, Culture and Identity / Promoting Healthy Eating in Early Years Settings / Multi-disciplinary Working /

March 2008   176 pages

Paperback (978-1-4129-4722-0) £17.99 Hardcover (978-1-4129-4721-3) £60.00

nd out more and order online at

www.sagepub.co.uk

Improving Services for Young Children
From Sure Start to Children's Centres

Angela Anning & Mog Ball

University of Leeds, UK

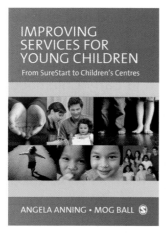

`In this excellent book two of the principal investigators from the huge national evaluation of Sure Start bring together key findings of "what works" as the local programmes are turned into children's centres and rolled out across England. Chapters on all aspects of Sure Start and children's centres reflect the services themselves in providing a valuable "one stop shop" for those who want to understand how to work effectively with young children and their parents' - **Dame Gillian Pugh, Visiting Professor, Institute of Education, University of London**

Contents

What was Sure Start and why did it matter? / *Part 1: Establishing appropriate sites for service delivery; Effective communication and engagement* / Getting Started / Buildings / *Part 2: The ethics of social engineering and intervening in peoples' lives* / Ethnicity / Empowering parents / *Part 3: Children's and young person's development; Supporting transitions; Multi- agency teamwork* / Maternity Services / Early Learning, Play and Childcare / Speech and Language Development/ Employability for Parents / *Part 4: Safeguarding and promoting the welfare of children; Sharing information* / Parenting Programmes / Domestic Violence / Lessons for Children's Centres

May 2008   192 pages
Paperback (978-1-4129-4822-7) £21.99   Hardcover (978-1-4129-4821-0) £65.00

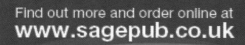

Communication, Language and Literacy from Birth to Five

Avril Brock & Carolynn Rankin

Leeds Metropolitan University

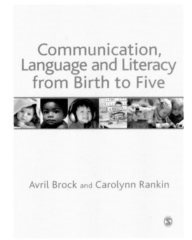

`A delightful and reader-friendly publication for students of early education to learn basic concepts in language acquisition and literacy, this book offers a plethora of ideas for teaching and assessment of language development while displaying a sensitivity to teaching a diverse population of young children. A wealth of information about how books, storytelling, drama and the arts enhance children's language and literacy skills is shared throughout the text' - ***Professor Louise Swiniarski, Education Department, Salem State College, MA, USA***

Contents

April 2008   144 pages

Paperback (978-14129-4590-5) £17.99   Hardcover (978-14129-4589-9) £60.00

Behaviour Management with Young Children
Crucial First Steps with Children 3-7 years

Bill Rogers & Elizabeth McPherson
Victoria, Australia

`What a privilege to read a book written by the person that has had the most impact on my classroom teaching and the whole ethos of our school. *Behaviour Management with Young Children* brings together Bill's insight into behaviour management and Elizabeth's understanding of young children and has resulted in a practical and realistic behaviour management manual that will be easily accessible to teachers in the early years...I shall be recommending it to all my teaching and support staff as essential reading' - **Debbie Hoy, Headteacher, Brookland Infant & Nursery School, Cheshunt, Hertfordshire**

Contents

The critical first days and first week / Transition to on-task learning time / Developing a whole-class student behaviour agreement / Developing a teacher management plan / Helping students manage their behaviour / Children with special behaviour needs / Working with parents using the classroom behaviour agreement

April 2008   176 pages

Paperback (978-1-8478-7364-4) £18.99   Hardcover (978-1-8478-7363-7) £60.00